The Struggle

Combat with the Self

Imam Sayyid Ruhollah Khomeini

AL-BURĀQ

Heighten The Mind

Copyright

ISBN: 978-9-64335-557-9.

Printed and published by al-Burāq Publications.

Ordering Information
We offer discounts and promotions for wholesale purchases and for non-profit organizations, libraries, and other educational institutions. Contact us at the email below for further information.

www.al-Buraq.org
publications@al-Buraq.org

First Edition | December 2003
Second Edition | December 2021

Dedication

The publication of this book was made possible through the generous support of our donors.

Please recite *Sūrah al-Fātiha* and ask Allāh for the Divine reward (*thawāb*) to be conferred upon the donors and the souls of all those in whose memory their loved ones have contributed graciously towards the publication of *The Greatest Struggle: Combat with the Self.*

Duaa al-Hujja

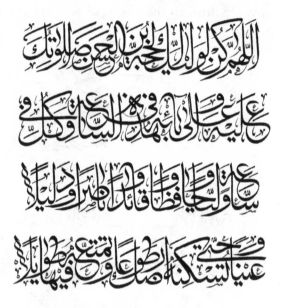

O Allah, be, for Your representative, the Hujjat (proof), son of al-Hasan, Your blessings be upon him and his forefathers, in this hour and in every hour: a guardian, a protector, a leader, a helper, a proof, and an eye until You make him live on the Earth, in obedience (to You), and cause him to live in it for a long time.

Table of Contents

Preface

بِسْمِ اللهِ الرَّحْمٰنِ الرَّحِيمِ

In the Name of Allāh, the Most Gracious,
the Most Merciful

The ordinary man normally has a one-dimensional personality, but great people who are truly liberated, such as the prophets and friends of Allah, have personalities of several aspects. Sometimes it is difficult or even impossible for an ordinary person's intellect to grasp how these various dimensions can be encompassed in the existence of such great people. As an outstanding religions figure, Imam Khomeini may be included among such great personalities. In addition to his leadership abilities, political insight and far sightedness, he now also may be considered to be a distinguished teacher of Islamic ethics. For various reasons, this aspect of his personality has not become very well known. This book is composed of some of his lectures on morals, which were delivered prior to the victory of the Islamic Revolution during the period of his exile in Najaf. He invites all, especially the students of divinity, to refinement of the soul, asceticism and piety.

This is a work in morals, in Farsi and Arabic, *akhlaq*. It is not a philosophical work, but a moral exhortation directed toward the seminary students of Najaf, and toward the institution of the seminary, or *hawzah 'ilmi*, as well. The work reveals the moral sensitivity of Imam Khomeini, his paternal anxiety regarding the seminarians and his dedication to the institution of the seminary. Upon reading this work one will discover that along with revolutionary fervor and condemnation of foreign imperialism there can be found a mystic's taste for spiritual devotions. The waters of *'irfan* (gnosis) run deep in the thought of Imam Khomeini and nourish his moral outlook. This work is a testimony to the truth of Shahid Mutahhari's remark that *'irfan* and ethics are both concerned with the improvement of character, but from different perspectives. In ethical works one finds a description of virtues and vices and moral prescriptions and proscriptions, while in *'irfani* works one finds a description of a process through which the soul moves toward Allah and acquires virtues corresponding to the divine attributes along the way. The way of moral reform advocated by Imam Khomeini is a process of spiritual development in which the adept learns to conquer and then loose interest in his worldly desires and become totally devoted to God. This process is described as a journey toward Allah, a journey which holds a central place in *'irfan*, which may be considered the kernel of Islam. This journey is described in different ways and from a variety of viewpoints in the poetry of the Sufis, in the transcendent philosophy of Mulla Sadra, and in the poetry and teachings of Imam Khomeini, as well.

Although the present work consists of speeches delivered to the students at Najaf, the moral advice given is particularly pertinent for all Muslims in the contemporary situation of discord and confusion. Imam Khomeini advises the seminarians to abandon their quarreling, which only serves as an opportunity for mischief on the part of the enemies of Islam. In the Islamic world today, we also observe that the opponents of the Islamic movement take advantage of disputes among Muslims. Imam reminds the students that they do not possess sufficient wealth and power to make these things worth fighting over even according to the standards of materialism. Parallel remarks are appropriate for the Muslim world as a whole, given the poverty and powerlessness which characterize the vast masses of the Islamic ummah. Imam sanctions the students that they should take heed of the fact that the major purpose of the prophets and the Imams has been spiritual progress and moral improvement, and that the students must not content themselves with learning a few terms of Islamic jurisprudence. The same warning should be heeded by contemporary Muslims. We must not content ourselves with a handful of slogans and the performance of a few rituals, but must take steps for spiritual and moral growth. Not merely in the seminary of Najaf, but wherever and to whom ever Islam is taught, this teaching must not confine itself to a rehearsal of basic beliefs and necessary practices, but must be accompanied by the moral and spiritual teachings which were the primary focus of the prophets and the Imams, peace be upon them.

The present work may be read from a number of different perspectives. It may be read in order to gain insight into the thought of the founder of the Islamic Revolution of Iran. It may be read in order to become familiar with the sort of problems which existed in Najaf at thetime the lectures were delivered. It can be read as an example of the type of moral preaching which could be expected from the among the best of Shi'ite moral teachers of this age. It is a work which can be read in order to learn something about history, sociology or anthropology, and in all of these areas valuable lessons are to be learned. But more important than any of these is the moral lessons to be drawn for the Islamic community in general. Let us not content ourselves with ritual duties while ignoring the need for moral reform. Let us appoint moral guides in all of our Islamic educational institutions, so that Islamic education may become more truly a training in submission to Allah, and let us draw upon the example as well as the teachings of the prophets and the Imams so that we may learn to seek to commence the journey of the believer toward Allah, *in sha' Allah*!

The remainder of this introduction consists of a few biographical remarks with particular reference to the moral and spiritual training of Imam Khomeini, may he rest in peace.

Ruhollah Musawi Khomeini, was born in 1902 in the town of Khomayn, which is about half way between Tehran and the southwestern city of Ahwaz. Ruhollah's father and grandfather were religious scholars in Khomayn. His father, Ayatollah Mustafa, is said to have been murdered by bandits when Ruhollah was less than six months old. His mother, Hajar, was the daughter of the religious scholar Aqa Mirza Ahmad Mujtahed Khuansari. The boy was raised by his mother and an aunt, both of whom died of cholera when he was six. His education was then supervised by his older brother, Ayatollah Pasandida. At nineteen, Ruhollah travelled northwest from Khomayn to the city of Arak, wherehe became a student of Sheikh Abd al-Karim Ha'eri, a leading religious scholar of his day. The following year, Sheikh Ha'eri and his student Ruhollah moved to Qom, where the Sheikh reorganized and revitalized the entire institution of religious education in that city, which was already famous as a center of learning. Ruhollah studied in Qom until the death of Sheikh Ha'eri, in 1936, after which he began teaching theology, ethics, philosophy and mysticism. It was during his first fourteen years in Qom that Ayatollah Khomeini became familiar with the intertwined traditions of philosophy and mysticism which flourished during Iran's Safawid period (16th and 17th centuries) and which continue to exert an enormous influence on contemporary Shi'ite thought.

When he arrived in Qom, Imam Khomeini began to receive private instruction in ethics with Hajj Mirza Jawad Maleki Tabrizi, the author of a book entitled, *The Secrets of Prayer (Asrar al-Salat)*. Imam Khomeini also wrote a book on this topic, called *The Secret of Prayer: Prayers of the Gnostics or Ascension of the Wayfarers (Sirr al-Salat: Salat al-'Arefin ya Mi'raj al-Salikin)*. His instruction under Mirza Jawad continued until the death of the teacher, in 1925. Imam Khomeini also studied the mystic tradition from Hajj Mirza Abu al-Hassan Rafi'i Qazvini, who was in Qom from 1923 until 1927. Qazvini is known for his commentary on a supplication which is recited daily in the pre-dawn hours during the month of Ramadan. Later, Imam Khomeini would also write a commentary on this prayer. Finally, and perhaps most importantly among his spiritual guides, there was Aqa Mirza Muhammad Ali Shahabadi, the author of *Spray from the Seas (Rashahat al-Bahar)*, who was in Qom from 1928 to 1935. In the mystic tradition of which Shahabadi was a part, the phrase 'spray from the sea' may be taken as a symbol for inspiration from God. It was with Shahabadi that Imam Khomeini is reported to have studied the *Fusus al-Hikam (Bezels of Wisdom)* of Ibn al-Arabi (d. 1240) and the important commentary on that work by Qaysari (d. 1350).

In 1929, Imam Khomeini married, and a year later his first son, Mustafa, was born. Over the course of the years, two other sons and four daughters were born. Mustafa would grow up to be killed in Iraq by agents of the Shah. The youngest son, Sayyid Ahmad, would become a secretary to his father, and afterward, a political leader in his own right.

Recalling his years as a student in Qom, Imam Khomeini himself has publicly commented on the hostility toward mysticism and philosophy which was to be found in certain quarters in Qom, feelings which are still harbored by some members of the clergy. The story is often repeated that when Imam had begun teaching philosophy in Qom and his first son was a small child, some seminarians felt it necessary to perform a ritual cleansing of a cup from which the child had drunk water because of his impurity as the son of a teacher of philosophy! Imam reports that his teacher, Shahabadi, sought to oppose this hostility by making people familiar with the doctrines of the mystics so they could see for themselves that there was nothing inimical to Islam in the teachings of the gnostics:

Once a group of merchants came to see the late Shahabadi (may God have mercy on him), and he began to speak to them on the same mystical topics that he taught to everyone. I asked him whether it was appropriate to speak to them of such matters and he replied: "Let them be exposed just once to these heretical teachings! I too now find it incorrect to divide people into categories and pronounce some incapable of understanding these matters."

One of the most dramatic efforts of Imam Khomeini to bring mysticism to the people occurred after the Islamic Revolution with his Lectures on *Surat al-Fatiha* from which the above report has been quoted. After the Revolution, there were televised lessons on the interpretation of the Qur'an by Ayatollah Taleqani. When Ayatollah Taleqani died on September 10, 1979, about a half year after the victory of the revolution, the televised commentary on the Qur'an was taken up by a younger scholar. Imam Khomeini suggested that a more senior authority might be sought for the program. After consulting among themselves, those responsible for the broadcast decided to request that Imam himself provide the commentary. Imam responded that if the cameras could be brought to his residence he would comply with the request. The result was the Lectures on *Surat al-Fatiha*, a stunning mystical interpretation of the opening verses of the Qur'an, in which one of the dominant themes was the claim that the whole world is a name of God. In these lectures Imam also contends that the philosophers of Islam, the mystics and the poets have used different terminologies to express the same insights, and he urges his viewers not to reject what is taught by members of these groups until they understand what is being expressed, even if the language used raises suspicions of heterodoxy. Thus, Imam's preaching in this area was very much a plea for tolerance.

Imam Khomeini's emphasis on tolerance was not limited to mysticism and poetry. Imam Khomeini's teacher in Islamic jurisprudence, Sheikh Ha'eri, was succeeded in Qom by

Ayatollah Borujerdi, who came to be recognized as the supreme authority on the subject. After the death of Ayatollah Borujerdi, in 1961, Imam Khomeini came to be recognized as one of several supreme experts in Islamic jurisprudence, a *marja-e taqlid.* In this role, Imam Khomeini issued a number of decrees which were looked upon with suspicion by more conservative clerics. Many of the religious scholars in both Sunni and Shi'ite legal schools have ruled that music and chess are forbidden activities. Imam Khomeini ruled that some forms of music are permissible and playing chess is not contrary to Islamic law. As a result, interest in traditional Iranian music has thrived since the Revolution. Imam Khomeini also encouraged women to play an expanded role in society, to the chagrin of more conservative interpreters of Islamic law.

To Western observers it may seem paradoxical that the very same man who preached tolerance with respect to the perceived challenges to orthodoxy posed by philosophy, mysticism, poetry and music, should also have been so intolerant toward the proponents of Westernization, toward the form of Marxism propagated in the name of Islam by the People's Mojahedin Organization of Iran (PMOI), and toward those who, like Salman Rushdie, would insult the Prophet of Islam or his family. The apparent contradiction is removed once it is recognized that Imam Khomeini did not value tolerance for its own sake, but for the sake of Islam. Central to Imam Khomeini's understanding of Islam is gnosis, *'irfan*. In Sunni Islam, the exoteric and esoteric dimensions of religion have been kept largely distinct, with the esoteric mostly confined to the Sufi orders. In Shi'ite Islam, there has been a long tradition in which many of the practices and teachings of the Sufis have been integrated into the religious life and thought of an important segment of the official clergy. This form of mysticism, or gnosis, draws upon the Sufi theory of Ibn al-Arabi, the philosophical mysticism of Sadr al-Din Shirazi (d. 1640) and Hadi Sabzawari (d. 1878), both of whom were Shi'ite clerics, and the poetic expression of mysticism by Molawi Jalal al-Din Rumi (d. 1273) and Hafez (d. 1391). The poetry is often set to music.

Because of political and religious repression, those involved in 'irfan often had to keep their teachings underground. Imam Khomeini, in line with the sentiments his reports having been expressed by his teacher Shahabadi, sought to initiate a process through which 'irfan could become public. This process was not to be a sudden revolution. His own works on 'irfan were not very widely distributed during his lifetime, but a persistent emphasis on the mystical elements of Shi'ite thought were interspersed among the more popular political declarations, and may be found in *The Greatest Jihad*, aswell.

The revolutionary Islamic movement led by Imam Khomeini may even be viewed as the exoteric dimension of the impetus to reveal Islamic mysticism to the public. The Islamic revolution was a means to bring Islam into public life, from which it was being marginalized during the reign of the Shah. The process of making Islam central to public life was also resisted by conservative religious groups, who saw in this movement a departure from tradition. Imam Khomeini argued that the guardian jurist of Islamic law had the authority to modify the traditional understanding of the law in order to protect the Islamic order.

Conservatives would argue that any break from tradition could only bring deviation from Islamic order. The kind of judgment required by Imam Khomeini's vision of Islamic government is one which goes beyond what is provided for in traditional discussions of Islamic jurisprudence. It is a kind of wisdom, however, which can be expected of the 'perfect man', the *insan kamil*, the goal of personal development in the mystic tradition.

An example of the way in which his political awareness demanded a tolerance not found among more conservative clerics may be found in his attitudes toward Sunni Islam. In traditional Shi'ite circles it would not be considered permissible for a Shi'ite to stand behind a Sunni prayerleader. Imam Khomeini ruled that such prayer was valid, and even himself publicly participated in ritual prayer behind a Sunni cleric.

Thus, the flexibility and tolerance which characterize Imam Khomeini's thought do not stem from the libertarian element in Islamic thought, but from a commitment to a movement from the esoteric to the exoteric dimensions of Islamic life, a movement which demanded the implementation of Islamic law as well as the propagation of mystical ideas.

Imam Khomeini's attitudes toward mysticism and politics are especially well illustrated by his invitation to President Gorbachev to embrace Islam. On January 3, 1988, Imam Khomeini sent a delegation to Moscow led by Ayatollah Jawadi Amuli who presented Imam's letter of invitation to President Gorbachev. In the letter, Imam congratulated Gorbachev for his admission of the failures of communism, and he suggested that the Soviet leader consider the alternative to communist ideology posed by Islam. In order to acquaint the Russian leader with Islam, Imam Khomeini recommended the works of the philosophers Farabi and Ibn Sina (Avicenna), and the mystic, Ibn al-'Arabi. Conservative clerics were incensed that Imam should choose to represent Islamic thought through the works of philosophers and a Sufi, instead of works of jurisprudence and traditional devotional literature. President Gorbachev politely declined the invitation to convert, although he said that he would consider the importance of spiritual values in society. Imam Khomeini appears to have been genuinely disappointed that the response was not affirmative, and when a Soviet delegate read Gorbachev's reply to Imam Khomeini in Tehran, Imam repeatedly interrupted with criticism of the views expressed in the letter. Such unconventional diplomacy demonstrates Imam's commitment to Islamic mysticism and its propagation, despite criticism from the clergy which he championed. It also provides an indication of the unusual way in which mysticism and politics were combined in the thinking of Imam Khomeini.

Imam wrote several works which treated mystical topics, or which treated topics in a way characteristic of the mystical tradition. Their titles are suggestive: Commentary on the Supplication Before Dawn (Sharh al-Du'a al-Sahar), The Lamp of Guidance to

Vicegerency and Guardianship (Misbah al-Hidayat ala al-Khalifat wa al-wilayah), The Countenance of Allah (Liqa' Allah), The Secret of Prayer: Prayers of the Gnostics or Ascension of the Wayfarers (Sirr al-Salat: Salat al-'Arefin ya Mi'raj al-Salikin), Annotation to the Commentary on 'The Bezels of Wisdom' (Ta'liqat ala Sharh al-Fusus al-Hikam), Annotation to the Commentary on 'The Lamp of Intimacy' (Ta'liqat ala Sharh al-Misbah al-Uns), two books of commentaries and annotations to another commentary on a collection of reports regarding the Prophet and Imam's called Ras al-Jalut, Lectures on Surat al-Fatiha, Marginalia to 'The Journeys' (Hashiyeh ala al-Asfar), Etiquette of Prayer (Adab al-Salat), Commentary on Forty Sayings of the Prophet and Imams (Chehel Hadith).

After he became a *marja-e taqlid*, political events dominated the life of Imam Khomeini. In 1963, the Shah's forces massacred thousands who protested against the dictatorship. Imam Khomeini was arrested for his inflammatory speeches and was taken to Tehran. Later he was released with the announcement that he had agreed to refrain from further political activity. He denied that he had made any such agreement and was picked up again. He was taken to an unknown destination by car. When the car turned off the main highway, it is reported that Imam imagined that he would be assassinated in a remote quarter of the desert. He felt his heart to see if it was racing, but found that it was calm. He narrated that he was never afraid. He was taken to a small airstrip where a plane waited to take him to exile in Turkey. The following year his place of exile was changed to the shrine city of Najaf in southern Iraq. Imam Khomeini remained in Najaf for fourteen years, and it was during these years that the lectures collected under the title, *Jihad al-Akbar* were delivered. In 1978, the Shah put pressure on the Baathist government in Iraq to expel Ayatollah Khomeini. After being refused asylum at the airport in Kuwait, Imam commented that he would spend his life traveling from one airport to another, but that he would not be keep silence. Finally, he was admitted to

France, where he resided at Neauphle-le-Chateaux, outside Paris. In February 1979, he returned triumphantly to Iran and the Islamic Republic was launched.

Imam Khomeini was revered for the simplicity of his lifestyle and for his rigorous attention to even supererogatory details of Islamic ritual. He is said to have always faced Mecca when he performed his ablutions. He preferred to purchase the least expensive shoes. If he drank half a glass of water, he would put a piece of paper over it to keep the dust out and save the rest for later. Some claim that he had a special relation with the twelfth Imam, the Mahdi, Peace be upon him, the awaited one who will defeat injustice prior to the final judgment. Such claims are also a part of the mystical tradition of Shi'ite Islam.

The Greatest Jihad: Combat with the Self

Yet another year of our lives has passed. You young people are advancing toward old age, and we old people toward death. During this academic year you have become aware of the extent of your learning and study. You know how much you have acquired and how high the edifice of your education has been raised. However, with respect to the refinement of virtue, the acquisition of religious manners, divine learning and purification of the soul, what have you done? What positive steps have you taken? Have you had any thought of refinement or self-reformation? Have you had any program in this field? Unfortunately, I must submit that you have not done anything striking, and that with regard to the reformation and refinement of the self you have not taken any great steps.

Recommendations for the Seminaries of Religious Learning

Simultaneous with the study of scholarly matters, the seminaries of religious learning are in need of teaching and learning in morals and spirituality. It is necessary to have moral guides, trainers for the spiritual abilities, and sessions for advice and counseling. Programs in ethics and moral reform, classes in manners and refinement, instruction in divine learning, which are the principle aim of the mission of the prophets, Peace be with them, must be officially instituted in the seminaries. Unfortunately, scant attention is paid in the centers of learning to these essential issues. Spiritual studies are declining, so that in the future the seminaries will not be able to train scholars of ethics, refined and polished counselors, or godly men. Occupation with discussion and inquiry into elementary problems does not allow the opportunity for the basic and fundamental topics which are instances of the favors of the Noble Qur'an and of the great Prophet (S) and the other prophets and saints (*'awliya*), Peace be with them. The great jurist-consults and highranking professors, who are noteworthy in the scholarly community, had better try, in the course of their lessons and discussions, to train and refine people and to be more concerned with spiritual and ethical topics. For the seminary students it is also necessary that in their efforts to acquire erudition and refinement of the soul that they give sufficient weight to their important duties and momentous responsibilities.

Recommendations for the Seminary Students

You who today are studying in these seminaries, and who shall tomorrow take charge of the leadership and guidance of society, do not imagine that your only duty is to learn a handful of terms, for you have other duties as well. In these seminaries you must build and train yourselves so that when you go to a city or village you will be able to guide the people there and show them refinement. It is expected that when you depart from the center for the study of religious law, you yourselves will be refined and cultivated, so that you will be able to cultivate the people and train them according to Islamic ethical manners and precepts. If, God forbid, you were not to reform yourselves in the center of learning, and you were not to realize spiritual ideals, then—may Allah protect us—everywhere you went, people would be perverted, and you would have given them a low opinion of Islam and of the clergy.

You have a heavy responsibility. If you do not fulfill your duty in the seminaries, if you do not plan your refinement, and if you merely pursue the learning of a few terms and issues of law and jurisprudence, then God protect us from the damage that you might cause in the future to Islam and Islamic society. It is possible, may Allah protect us, for you to pervert and mislead the people. If due to your actions, deeds and unfair behavior, one person looses his way and leaves Islam, you would be guilty of the greatest of the major sins, and it would be difficult for your repentance to be accepted. Likewise, if one person finds guidance, then according to a narration: "it is better than all upon which the sun doth shine."[1] Your responsibility is very heavy. You have duties other than those of the laity. How many things are permissible for the laity, which are not allowed for you, and may possibly be forbidden! People do not expect you to

---

[1] The Commander of the Faithful, Imam Ali, Peace be with him, said: When the Messenger of Allah, may the Peace and Blessings of Allah be with him and with his progeny, sent me to Yemen, he said: O Ali! Do not fight against anyone until you invite him to Islam. I swear by Allah, if by your hand the Great and Almighty Allah may guide a man, then it is better for you than all that the sun rises upon or sets upon, and you are his *wali* (guardian). *Kafi*, Vol. 5, p. 36, "The Book of Struggle", "Section on Invitation to Islam prior to Fighting," hadith 2.

perform many permissible deeds, to say nothing of low unlawful deeds, which if you were to perform them, God forbid, people would form a bad opinion of Islam and of the clerical community.

The trouble is here: if the people witness your actions as contrary to what is expected, they become deviated from religion. They turn away from the clergy, not from an individual. If only they would turn away from just one person, and form a low opinion of just that person! But if they see an unbecoming action contrary do decorum on the part of a single cleric, they do not examine it and analyze it, that at the same time among businessmen there are unrighteous and perverted people, andamong office workers corruption and ugly deeds may be seen, so it is possible that among the clergy there may also be one or more impious or deviant persons. Hence, if a grocer does something wrong, it is said that such and such a grocer is a wrongdoer. If a druggist is guilty of an ugly deed, it is said that such a druggist is an evildoer. However, if a preacher performs an unbecoming act, it is not said that such and such a preacher is deviant, it is said that preachers are bad!

The responsibilities of the learned are very heavy; the 'ulama have more duties than other people. If you review the chapters related to the responsibilities of the 'ulama in *'Usul Kafi* and *Wassa'il*,[2] you will see how they describe the heavy responsibilities and serious obligations of the learned. It is narrated that when the soul reaches the throat, there is no longer any chance for repentance, and in that state one's repentance will not be accepted, although God accepts the repentance of the ignorant until the last minute of their lives.[3] In another narration it is reported that seventy

---

[2] *Usul Kafi,* "Book of the Virtue of Knowledge" *(Kitab Fadl al-'Ilm),* Chapters: *"bab sifat al-'ulama", "bab badh al-'ilm", "bab al-nahy 'an al-qawl bi ghayr 'ilm", "bab isti'mal al-'ilm", "bab al-musta'kil bi 'ilmihi wa al-mubahi bihi", "bab luzum al-hujjah 'ala al-'alim", "bab al-nawadir", and Wasa'il al Shi'a, vol. 18, pp. 9-17, 98-129, "kitab al-qada",* Chapters: *"abwab sifat alqadi", bab 4, 11, 12.*

[3] Jamil ibn Durraj says that he heard from Imam Sadiq, Peace be with him, that he said, "When the soul reaches here (and with his hand he pointed to his neck) for the learned there remains no further chance of repentance." Then he recited this ayah: "The repentance of Allah is only for those who do evil in ignorance." (4:17). *Usul Kafi,* Vol. 1, p. 59, "The Book of the Virtue of Knowledge", "Chapter on the Requirement for an *'Alim* to bring proof... ", hadith 3.

sins will be forgiven of one who is ignorant before one sin is forgiven of a *'alim*.[4] This is because the sin of an *'alim* is very harmful to Islam and to Islamic society. If a vulgar and ignorant person commits a sin, he only wins misfortune for himself. However, if an *'alim* becomes deviant, if he becomes involved in ugly deeds, he perverts an entire world (*'alam*). He has injured Islam and the *'ulama* of Islam.[5]

There is also a narration according to which the people of hell suffer from the stench of an *'alim* whose deeds do not accord with his

---

[4] Hafs ibn Qiyyas said that Imam Sadiq, Peace be with him, said: "O Hafs! Seventy sins will be forgiven of an ignorant person before on sin is forgiven of an *'alim*." *Usul Kafi*, Vol. 1, p. 59, The Book of the Virtue of Knowledge, Chapter of the Requirement of an *'Alim* for proof.

[5] The Prophet of Allah, may the Peace and Blessings of Allah be with him and with his progeny, said, "There are two groups from my community such that if they are righteous then the community will be righteous, and if they are corrupt, then the community will become corrupt." It was asked, "Who are they?" He replied, "The *'ulama* and the rulers." *Khisal*, [by Shaykh alSaduq], The Second Chapter, p.37; *Tuhaf al'Uqul*, p. 50.

knowledge.[6] For this very reason, in this world there is a great difference between an *'alim* and an ignorant person with regard to benefit and injury to Islam and to the Islamic community. If an *'alim* is deviant, it is possible that the community will become infected by deviation. And if a *'alim* is refined, and he observes the morality and manners of Islam, he will refine and guide the community. In some of the towns to which I went during the summer, I saw that the people of *a town* were well mannered with religious morals. The point is this, that they had an *'alim* who was righteous and pious. If an *'alim* who is pious and righteous lives in a community, town or state, his very existence will raise the refinement and guidance of the people of that realm, even if he does not verbally

---

[6] Sulaym ibn Qays Hilali said that he heard from the Commander of the Faithful, Peace be with him, that he reported from the Prophet, that he said, "There are two kinds of *'ulama*, one who acts in accordance with his knowledge, so he has been saved, and the *'alim* who does not act in accordance with his knowledge, so he will perish. And truly the people of hell will suffer from the stench of the *'alim* who does not act in accordance with his knowledge." *Usul Kafi*, Vol. 1, p. 55, The Book of the Virtue of Knowledge, Chapter on the Application of Knowledge, hadith 1.

propagate and guide.[7] We have seen people whose existence causes lessons to be learned, merely seeing them and looking at them raises one's awareness.

At present in Tehran, about which I have some information, the neighborhoods differ from one another. Neighborhoods in which a pure and refined *'alim* lives have righteous people with strong faith. In another neighborhood where a corrupt deviant person wears the turban, and has become the prayer leader, and set up shop, you will see that the people there have been misled, and have been polluted and perverted. This is the same pollution from the stench of which the people of hell suffer. This is the same stench which the evil *'alim*, the *'alim* without action, the perverted *'alim* has brought in this world, and the smell of it causes the people of hell to suffer. It is not because something is added to him there, that which occurs to this *'alim* in the next world is something which has been prepared in this

---

[7] Imam Sadiq, Peace be with him, said, "Invite the people to excellence, but not by your tongue, rather let people see in you right struggle (*ijtihad*), truthfulness and piety."

world. Nothing is given to us except that which we have done. If an *'alim* is corrupt and evil, he corrupts the society, although in this world we are not able to smell the stench of it. However, in the next world the stench of it will be perceived. But a vulgar person is not able to bring such corruption and pollution into the Islamic society. A vulgar person would never allow himself to proclaim that he was an Imam or the Mahdi, to proclaim himself a prophet, or to have received revelation. It is a corrupt *'alim* who corrupts the world: "If an *'alim* is corrupt, a world (*'alam*) is corrupted."[8]

---

[8] *Ghurar al-Hikam*, Vol. 7, p. 269.

Importance in Refinement & Purification of the Soul

Those who have constructed [their own] religions, causing the straying and deviation of masses of peoples, have for the most part been scholars. Some of them even studied and disciplined themselves in the centers of learning.[9] The head of one of the heretical sects studied in these very seminaries of ours. However, since his learning was not accompanied by refinement and purification, since he did not advance on the path toward God, and since he did not remove the pollution from himself, he bore the fruit of ignominy. If man does not cast pollution from the core of his soul, not only will whatever studying and learning he does be of no benefit by itself, rather it will actually be harmful. When evil enters knowledge in this center, the product will be evil, root and branch, an evil tree. However much these

---

[9] This group includes Muhammad ibn Abd al-Wahhab (founder of the Wahhabi sect), Shaykh Ahmad Ahsa'i and Sayyid Kazim Rashti (founders of the Shaykhi sect), Ahmad Kasravi and Ghulam Ahmad (founder of the Qadiyani sect).

concepts are accumulated in a black impure heart, that which covers them will be greater. In a soul which is unrefined, knowledge is a dark cover: *Al-'ilm huwa al-hijab al-akbar* (Knowledge is the greatest cover).

Therefore, the vice of a corrupt *'alim* is greater and more dangerous forIslam than all vices. Knowledge is light, but in a black corrupt heart it spreads wide the skirts of darkness and blackness. A knowledge which would draw a man closer to God, in a worldly soul brings him far distant from the place of the Almighty. Even the knowledge of divine unity (*tawhid*), if it is for anything other than God, it becomes a cover of darkness, for it is a preoccupation with that which is other than God. If one memorizes and recites the Noble Qur'an in all fourteen different canonical methods of recital, if it is for anything other than God, it will not bring him anything but covering and distance from *Haqq ta'ala* (God). If you study, and go to some trouble, you may become a *'alim*, but you had better know that there is a big difference between being an *'alim* and being refined.

The late Shaykh,[10] our teacher, may Allah be pleased with him, said, "That which is said, 'How easy it is to become a mullah; how difficult it is to become a man,' is not correct. It should be said, 'How difficult it is to become a mullah, and it is impossible to become a man!'"

The acquisition of the virtues and human nobilities and standards is a difficult and great duty which rests upon your shoulders. Do not suppose now that you are engaged in studying the religious sciences, and learning *fiqh* (jurisprudence) which is the most honorable of these sciences, that you can take it easy otherwise, and that your responsibilities and duties will take care of themselves. If you do not have a pure intention of approaching God, these sciences

---

[10] Grand Ayatullah Hajj Shaykh Abd al-Karim Ha'eri Yazdi (d. 1355/ 1937), was one of the greatest of Islamic jurists and a source of imitation of the Shi'a in the fourteenth Islamic century. He attended the classes of masters such as Mirzaye Bozorg Shirazi, Mirza Muhammad Taqi Shirazi, Akhund Khorasani, Sayyid Kazim Yazdi, Sayyid Muhammad Isfahani Fesharaki, in Najaf and Samara. In the year 1340/1921, at the insistence of the *'ulama* of Qom and after finding a good omen in a passage from the Qur'an he took up residence in Qom and organized the Seminary of Qom. Among his works are, *Durar al-Fawa'id dar 'Usul, Al-Salah, AlNikah, Al-Rida', Al-Mawarith*, all in the field of jurisprudence.

will be of no benefit at all. If your studies, may Allah protect us, are not for the sake of God, and are for the sake of personal desires, the acquisition of position and the seats of authority, titles and prestige, then you will accumulate nothing for yourself but harm and disaster. This terminology you are learning, if it is for anything but God, it is harm and disaster.

This terminology, as much as it increases, it is not accompanied by refinement and fear of God (*taqwa*), then it will end in harm in this world and the next for the Muslim community. Merely knowing terminology is not effective. Even the knowledge of divine unity (*'ilm al-tawhid*) if it is not accompanied with purity of the soul, it will bring disaster. How many individuals have been *'ulama* with knowledge of monotheism, and have perverted whole groups of people. How many individuals have had the very same knowledge that you have, or even more knowledge, but were deviant and did not reform themselves, so that when they entered the community, they perverted many and led them astray.

This dry terminology, if it is not accompanied by piety (*taqwa*) and refinement of the soul, as much as it accumulates in one's mind it will only lead to the expansion of pride and conceit in the realm of the soul. The unfortunate *'alim* who is defeated by his own conceit cannot reform himself or his community, and it will result in nothing but harm to Islam and the Muslims. And after years of studying and wasting religious funding, enjoying his Islamic salary and fringe benefits, he will become an obstacle in the way of Islam and the Muslims. Nations will be perverted by him. The result of these lessons and discussions and the time spent in the seminary will be the prevention of the introduction to the world of Islam and the truths of the Qur'an; rather, it is possible that his existence will be barrier preventing the society from coming to know Islam and spirituality.

I am not saying that you should not study, that you should not acquire knowledge, but you have to pay attention, for if you want to be a useful and effective member of society and Islam and lead a nation to awareness of Islam and to defend the fundamentals of Islam, it is necessary that the basis of jurisprudence be strengthened and that you gain mastery of the subject. If, God forbid, you fail to study, then it is forbidden for you to remain in the seminary. You may not use the religious salary of the students of the religious sciences. Of course, the acquisition of knowledge is necessary, although in the same way that you take pains with the problems of *fiqh* and *'usul* (jurisprudence and its principles), you must make efforts in the path of self-reformation. Every step forward which you take in the acquisition of knowledge, should be matched by a step taken to beat down the desires of the soul, to strengthen one's spiritual powers, to acquire nobility of character, and to gain spirituality and piety (*taqwa*).

The learning of these sciences in reality is an introduction to the refinement of the soul and the acquisition of virtue, manners and divine knowledge. Do not spend your entire life with the introduction, so that you leave aside the conclusion. You are acquiring these sciences for the sake of a holy and high aim, knowing God and refining the self. You should make plans to realize the results and effects of your work, and you should be serious about reaching your fundamental and basic goal.

When you enter the seminary, before anything else, you should plan to reform yourselves. While you are in the seminary, along with your studies, you should refine yourselves, so that when you leave the seminary and become the leader of a people in a city or district, they may profit from you, take advice from you, and reform themselves by means of your deeds and manners and your ethical virtues. Try to reform and refine yourselves before you enter among the people. If now, while you are unencumbered, you do not reform yourselves, on the day when people come before you, you will not be able to reform yourselves.

Many things ruin people and keep them from studying and purifying themselves, and one of them, for some, is this very beard and turban! When the turban becomes a bit large, and the beard gets long, if one has not refined oneself, this can hinder one's studies, and restrict one. It is difficult to trample the commanding self under one's feet, and to sit at the feet of another for lessons. Shaykh Tusi,[11] may Allah have mercy on him, at the age of fifty-two would go to classes, while between the ages of twenty and thirty, he wrote some of his books! His *Tahdhib* was possibly written during this period.[12]

Yet at the age of fifty-two he attended the classes of the late Sayyid Murtada[13], may

---

[11] Abu Ja'far Muhammad ibn Hasan Tusi (385-460/995-1067). He is known as 'Shaykh al-Ta'ifah', and he was one of the most distinguished scholars of the Imami Shi'ah. He was the head of the jurists and theologians of his time, and he also was strong in literature, biography, exegesis, and hadith. His teachers were Shaykh Mufid, Sayyid Murtada, Ibn Ghada'iri, and Ibn 'Abdun. The Shaykh is the author of two famous books of Shi'ite hadiths, *Istibsar* and *Tahdhib*, and are counted among the four (most important) books of the Imami Shi'ah. Shaykh Tusi established Najaf as the center for Shi'ite learning.

[12] Shaykh Tusi began to write the *Tahdhib*, which is a commentary on the *Mughni'ah* of Shaykh Mufid, during the lifetime of his teacher (Shaykh Mufid, d. 413/1022). Shaykh Tusi was about twenty-six years old at this time.

[13] Ali ibn Husayn ibn Musa, known as Sayyid Murtada, and 'Alam alHuda (355-436/965-1044), is one of the greatest scholars of Islam and Shi'ism. Most of the great scholars of the Imami Shi'ah, including Shaykh Tusi, have benefited from his teaching. He wrote: *Amali, Al-Dhari'ah ila 'Usul al-Shari'ah, Al-Nasiriat, Al-Intisar, Al-Shafi.*

Allah have mercy on him, and thereby achieved a similar status as he did. God forbid that prior to acquiring good habits and strengthening one's spiritual powers that one's beard should turn a bit white and that his turban should get big, so that he would lose the blessings of knowledge and spirituality. So work, before your beards become white; before you gain the attention of the people, think about your state! God forbid that before a person develops himself, that people should pay heed to him, that he should become a personality and have influence among the people, causing him to loose his soul.

Before you loose hold of the reins of your self, develop and reform yourself! Adorn yourselves with good traits, and remove your vices! Become pure in your lessons and discussions, so that you may approach God! If one does not have good intentions, one will be kept far from the divine precincts. Beware that, after seventy years, when the book of your deeds is opened, Allah forbid that you should have been far from God the Almighty for seventy years. Have you heard the story of the 'stone' which was dropped into hell? Only after seventy years was the sound of its hitting the bottom of hell heard. According to a narration, the Prophet, may the Peace and Blessings of Allah be with him and with his progeny, said that it was an old man who died after seventy years, and during this seventy years he was falling into hell.[14] Be careful that in the seminary, by your own labor and the sweat of your brow during fifty years, more or less, that your do not thereby reach hell! You had better think! Make plans in the field of refinement and purification of the soul, and reformation of character.

Choose a teacher of morals for yourself; and arrange sessions for advice, counsel, and admonition. You cannot become refined by yourself. If there is no place in the seminary for moral counselors and sessions of advice and exhortation, it will be doomed to annihilation. How could it be that *fiqh* and *usul* (jurisprudence and its principles) should require teachers for lessons and discussions, and that for every science and skill a teacher

---

14 Fayd Kashani, *Kalamat Maknunah*, p. 123.

is necessary, and no one becomes an expert or learned in any specific field by being cocky and disdainful, yet with regard to the spiritual and ethical sciences, which are the goal of the mission of the prophets and are among the most subtle and exact sciences, they do not require teaching and learning, and one may obtain them oneself without a teacher! I have heard on numerous occasions that the late Shaykh Ansari,[15] was a student

---

[15] Shaykh Murtada Ansari (1214-1281/1799-1864), known as *Khatam alFuqaha wa al-Mujtahidin*, was one of the descendants of Jabir ibn Abd Allah Ansari, a Companion of the Prophet, may the Peace and Blessings of Allah be with him and with his progeny. He was a genius in the Principles of Jurisprudence (*'Ilm al-Usul*), and he brought great developments in this field. Some of his professors were: Shaykh Musa Kashif alGhita, Shaykh Ali Kashif al-Ghita, Mulla Ahmad Naraqi and Sayyid Muhammad Mujahid. Shaykh Ansari trained some great jurists, including: Akhund Khorasani, Mirza Shirazi and Mirza Muhammad Hasan Ashtiani. His works include: *Fara'id al-Usul* (known as *Rasa'il*) and *Makasib*, one of the most famous text books.

of a great Sayyid[16] who was a teacher of
ethics and spirituality. The prophets of God
were raised in order to train people, to
develop humanity, and to remove them from
ugliness, filth, corruption, pollution and
moral turpitude, and to acquaint them with
virtue and good manners: "I was raised in
order to complete noble virtue (*Makarim al-
Akhlaq*).[17] This knowledge which was
considered by God the Almighty to be so
important that He raised the prophets for it,
is not considered unfashionable in the
seminaries for our clergy. No one gives it
the importance of which it is worthy. Due to
the lack of spiritual and gnostic works in the
seminaries, material and worldly problems

---

[16] Sayyid Ali ibn Sayyid Muhammad (d.1283/1866), was one of the
great ascetics and mystics of his day. He received authorization (as
a *mujtahid*) from Shaykh Ansari and Sayyid Husayn, the Friday
Prayer leader of Shushtar. Sayyid Ali spent some time in Shushtar
as a judge and legal authority (*mufti*), and then moved to Najaf al-
Ashraf. There he attended the classes of Shaykh Ansari in *fiqh*.
And Shaykh Ansari also attended his classes in ethics. When
Shaykh Ansari passed away, Sayyid Ali was the executor of his
will and he succeeded him in his professorial position. The late
Shaykh Sayyid Ali was the professor and counselor of Akhund
Mulla Husaynqulli Hamadani, who had many students who were
led by him, some of the greatest of whom were: Mirza Javad
Malaki Tabrizi, Sayyid Ahmad Karbala'i, Shaykh Muhammad
Bihari, Sayyid Ali Qadi Tabrizi and Allamah Tabataba'i.

[17] *Majma' al-Bay'an*, under the exegesis of the fourth *ayah* of the
Surah, The Pen (*Qalam*).

have come so far as to penetrate the clergy (*ruhaniat*), and has kept many of them away from holiness and spirituality (*ruhaniat*), so that they do not even know what *ruhaniat* means, nor what the responsibilities of a cleric are and what kind of programs they should have. Some of them merely plan to learn a few words, return to their own localities, or somewhere else, and to grab facilities and position, and to wrestle with others [for them]. Like one who said: "Let me study *Sharh Lum'ah* and then I will know what to do with the village chief!" Do not be this way, that fromthe beginning you aim to win someone's position by studying, and that you intend to be the chief of some town or village. You may achieve your selfish desires and Satanic expectations, but for yourself and the Islamic community you will acquire nothing except harm and misfortune. Mu'awiyah was also chief for a long time, but for himself he achieved no result or benefit except curses and loathing and the chastisement of the life hereafter.

It is necessary for you to refine yourselves, so that when you become the chief of a community or a clan, you will be able to refine them, as well. In order to be able to take steps toward the reform and development of a community, your aim should be service to Islam and the Muslims. If you take steps for the sake of God, God the Almighty is the Turner of the hearts; He will turn hearts in favor of you: "Surely for those who believe and do good deeds, the Merciful (*al-Rahman*) will bring about love." (19:96) Take some trouble on the way to God, devote yourselves; God will not leave you unpaid, if not in this world, then in the next He will reward you. If, aside from Him, you have no reward in this world, what could be better? This world is nothing. This pomp and these personalities will come to an end after a few days, like a dream passes before the eyes of man, but the other worldly reward is infinite and never ending.

Warnings to the Seminaries

It is possible that by spreading poison and evil propaganda impure hands have portrayed ethical and reformatory programs as without importance, and have presented going to the *'mimbar'* (pulpit) for giving advice and making sermons as contrary to a scholarly station, and they inhibit the work of the great scholarly personalities who have the station of reforming and refining the seminaries by calling them *'mimbari'* (mere sermonizers). Today, in some seminaries, going to the *mimbar* and giving sermons may even be considered disgraceful! They forget that the Commander of the Faithful, Peace be with him, was *'mimbari'* (a sermonizer), and from the *mimbar* he would admonish people, make them aware of things, raise their consciousness, and guide them. Other Imams, Peace bewith them, were also this way.

Perhaps secret agents have injected this evil in order to exterminate spirituality and ethics in the seminaries, and as a result our seminaries have become corrupt and dissolute. God forbid that forming gangs, selfishness, hypocrisy and disagreements should penetrate the seminaries. The people of the seminaries fight with each other, they close ranks against one another, and they insult and belie one another. They become discredited in the Islamic community, so that the foreigners and enemies of Islam are able to get hold of the seminaries and destroy them. The ill-intentioned know that the country supports the seminaries, and as long as the country supports them it is not possible to beat them or tear them apart.

But on the day when the people of the seminaries and the student of the seminaries come to lack ethical principles and Islamic manners, and fight each other, and form opposing gangs, and are not refined and purified, dirty their hands with unsuitable deeds, then naturally the nation of Islam will get a bad impression of the seminaries and the clergy, and support for them will be lost, and consequently the way for the use of force and enemy influence will be opened. If you see that governments are afraid of a cleric and of a *marja'* (authority in Shi'ite jurisprudence and source of imitation), and take account of them, it is because of this, that they benefit from the support of the people, and in truth, they are afraid of the people. They consider it probable that if they show contempt and audacity and violate a cleric, that the people will rebel andrise up against them. However, if the clerics oppose one another and defame one another and do not behave with Islamic manners and morals, they will fall from their position in the community, and the people will abandon them.[18] The people expect you to be *ruhani* (spiritual, a cleric), well-mannered with the manners of Islam, and to be of the party of Allah. Restrain yourselves from the splendor and glitter of life and artificiality, and do not refuse any kind of self-sacrifice in the way of the advancement of Islamic ideals and service to the nation of Islam. Step forward on the way of God the Almighty to please Him, and except for the unique Creator pay attention to no one.

---

[18] Ali, Peace be with him, said: "If the bearers of *'ilm* (knowledge, science) bear it as it deserves to be borne, they will be loved by Allah, the angels, and those who are obedient to Him, and those who bear it for the sake of this world will be despised by Allah and held in contempt by the people." *Tuhaf al-'Uqul*, p. 201, Chapter on the words of the Commander of the Faithful, Peace be with him.

However, if, contrary to what is expected, it is seen that instead of paying attention to metaphysics, all you care about is this world, and just like the others you try to gain worldly and personal interests, and you fight with one another for the sake of the world and its base pleasures, and you take Islam and the Qur'an, may Allah forbid it, as playthings, simply to reach sinister goals and your own dirty, disgraceful and worldly intentions, and you turn your religion into a market place, then the people will be turned away and become cynical. So, you will be responsible. If some of those who wear the turban and burden the seminaries fight and brawl with each other and malign and slander one another because of personal grudges and the pursuit of worldly interests, and rivalry over some positions, they commit treason against Islam and the Qur'an and they violate the divine trust. God the Almighty has placed the holy religion of Islam in our hands as a trust. The noble Qur'an is a great divine trust. The 'ulama and ruhaniyun (clergy) are the bearers of the divine trust, and they bear the responsibility to protect that trust from betrayal. This stubbornness and personal and worldly antagonisms are treachery against Islam and the great Prophet of Islam.

I do not know what purpose is served by these oppositions, formations of cliques, and confrontations. If it is for the sake of the world, you do not have much of that! Supposing that you did benefit from pleasures and worldly interests, there would be no place for disagreements, unless you were not *ruhani* (spiritual, a cleric), and the only thing you inherited of *ruhaniat* (spirituality, being a cleric) was the robe and turban. A *ruhani* (a cleric) who is occupied with metaphysics, a *ruhani* who benefits from living teachings and reformative Islamic attributes, a *ruhani* who considers himself a follower of Ali ibn Abi Talib, Peace be with him, is not possibly tempted by the world, nor would he allow it to cause disagreements. You who have declared yourselves to be followers of the Commander of the Faithful, Peace be with him, you should at least make a bit of research into the life of that great man, and see if you are really one of his followers! Do you know and practice anything of his asceticism, *taqwa* (piety, God-wariness) and simple unadorned life? Do you know anything of that great man's combat against oppression and injustice, and class differences, and of his unhesitating defense and support of the oppressed and persecuted, of how he lent a hand to the dispossessed and suffering social classes? Have you put it into practice? Is the meaning of "Shi'ite" nothing more than the ornamental appearances of Islam?[19] Therefore, what is the difference between you and other Muslims, in virtue of which they are much further ahead and more advantageous than the Shi'a? What distinguishes you over them?

Those who today have set a part of the world on fire, who spill blood and who kill, do this because they are competing with each other in looting the nations of the world and swallowing their wealth and the products of

---

[19] *Sifat al-Shi'a*, written by Shaykh al-Saduq, and also Bihar al-Anwar, Vol. 65, pp. 83-95 and 149-196, "The Book of Faith and Infidelity", the section on, "Verily the Shi'ah are the people of the religion of Allah... ", the section on the Attributes of the Shi'ah and their kinds... " *Sharh-e Chehel Hadith*, Imam Khomeini (may he rest in Peace), hadith 29, translated by A. A. Qara'i as Forty Hadith: An Exposition, in the journal Al-Tawhid, Vol. X. [Tr.]

their labor, and in bringing the weak and underdeveloped countries under their dominion and control. Thus, in the name of freedom, development and prosperity, the defense of independence and protection of borders, and under other deceptive slogans, every day the flames of war are set in some corner of the world, and millions of tons of incendiary bombs are dropped upon nations without protection. This fighting seems correct and accords with the logic of worldly people whose brains are polluted. However, your conflicts, even according to their logic, are incorrect. If asked why they are fighting, they will say that they want to take over such and such a country; the wealth and income of such and such a country must be made ours. However, if you are asked why you have conflicts, and why you are fighting, what will be your answers? What benefit do you get from the world, for the sake of which you are fighting? Your monthly income, which the *marja'-e taqlid* (supreme authorities of religious jurisprudence) give to you, called *"shahriyah"*, is less than the money used by others for cigarettes! I saw in a newspaper or magazine, I don't recall exactly, that the amount the Vatican sends to a single priest in Washington is quite a large figure. I reckon it is more than that of the entire budget for all of the Shi'ite seminaries! Is it right for you, with your lifestyle and conditions, to have conflicts and confrontations with one another?

The root of all these conflicts which have no specific sacred aim is love of this world. If conflicts of this sort exist among you, it is for this reason, that you have not expelled the love of this world from your hearts. Because worldly interests are limited, each one rises up against his rival in order to obtain them. You desire a certain position, which someone else also wants, and naturally this leads to jealousy and strife. However, the people of God, who have expelled the love of this world from their hearts, have no aim but God, never fight with one another, and never cause such calamities and corruption. If all of the divine prophets were to gather in a city today, there would be no disagreement or conflict among them, for their aims and destinations are one. The hearts of all of them attend to God the Almighty, and they are clear of any love of this world.

If your deeds and actions, your way of life and your wayfaring are of this sort that is evident today, then you had better fear, may God protect us from it, that you may leave this world without being one of the Shi'a of Ali ibn Abi Talib, Peace be with him. You should fear that your repentance might not be accepted, and that the intercession of Imam Ali may be of no benefit to you. Before loosing the opportunity, you should try to remedy this. Give up these banal and shameful conflicts. These confrontations and conflicts are wrong. Do you compose two nations? Is your religion chauvinistic? Why will you not beware? Why are you not pure and honest and brotherly with one another? Why? Why?

These conflicts are dangerous, for they lead to corruption for which there is no compensation: the destruction of the seminaries; and it will make you worthless and dishonored in the community. This banding into gangs only is to your loss. Not only is it of no credit to you, but it brings dishonor and discredit to the community and the nation, and leads to the harm of Islam. If your oppositions to one another lead to corruption it will be an unforgettable offense and before God the Almighty it will be one of the greatest of all sins, because it will corrupt the community and make it wide open to the influence and domination of the enemy. Perhaps some hidden hands are at work spreading enmity and discord in the seminaries, by various means sowing the seeds of discord and strife poisoning the thoughts and confusing the minds, arranging for such things under the guise of 'religious duties', and by means of such religious duties corruption is established in the seminaries, so that by this means those who are useful for the future of Islam are destroyed and unable to serve Islam and the Islamic community in the future. It is necessary to be aware and conscious. Do not fool yourselves into thinking that your religious duties require such things, and that your religious obligations are such and so. Sometimes Satan determines responsibilities and duties for man. Sometimes selfish wants and desires force a man to do things in the name of religious duties. Offending a Muslim and saying something bad about a brother in faith are not a religious duties.

This is love of the world and love of self. These are the promptings of Satan which bring a dark day for man. This enmity is the enmity of the damned: *"That most surely is the truth, the contending of one with another of the inmates of the fire."* (38:64).

Enmity and contention exist in hell. The people of hell have conflicts, fighting and clawing at one another. If you have quarrels for the sake of this world, beware that you are preparing hell for yourself, and you are on the way there. There is no fighting for things of the other world. The people of the other world are pure and at peace with one another. Their hearts are overflowing with the love of God and servitude to Him. The love of God requires the love of those who have faith in God. The love for the servants of God is the shadow of that very love for God.

Do not set your own hands on fire. Do not set ablaze the flames of hell. Hell is lit with the ugly works and deeds of man. These are the deeds of refractory man which set this fire. It is narrated: "I passed hell when it was extinguished." If a man does not light the fire by his works and deeds, hell will be extinguished.[20] The interior of this disposition is hell. To approach this disposition is to approach hell. When man passes away from this world and the curtains are drawn aside, he will realize, *"This is for what your own hands have sent before,"* (3:182), *and "and what they had done they shall find present,"* (18:49). All of the deeds which are done by man in this world will be seen in the other world, and will be embodied for him, *"So he who has done an atom's weight of good shall see it and he who has done an atom's weight of evil shall see it."* (99:7-8). All of the works and deeds and words of man will be reflected in the other world. It is as if everything in our lives were

---

[20] This refers to a hadith according to which: "When some people asked our Imam about the inclusiveness of this *ayah ('And there is not one of you but shall come to it [hell]'* (19:71)), he replied, "We passed through hell and it was extinguished." *Ilm Yaqin*, Vol. 2, p. 917.

being filmed, and in that world the film will be shown, and one will be able to deny none of it. All of our actions and movements will be shown to us, in addition to the testimony given by our limbs and organs: *"They shall say: 'Allah Who makes everything speak, has made us speak.'"* (41:21).

Before God, Who will make all things able to speak and bear witness, you will not be able to deny your ugly deeds or hide them. Think a little, look ahead, weigh the consequences of your deeds, keep in mind the perilous events which take place after death, the pressure of the grave, the world of *barzakh* (the period between death and resurrection), and do not neglect the difficulties which will follow that. At least believe in hell. If a man believes in the perilous events which take place after death, he will change his way of life. If you had faith and certainty in these things, you would not live so freely and licentiously. You will try to guard your pen, your steps, and your tongue, in order to reform and purify yourselves.

Divine Blessings

Because He favors His servants, God the Blessed and Supreme gavethem intellect, He gave them the power to refine and purify themselves, He sent the prophets and *'awliya* (the friends of God) to guide people and to help them to reform themselves so that they do not fall into the severe chastisement of hell. If these preventatives do not cause the awareness and refinement of man, God, the Merciful, will make him aware through other means: by various difficulties, afflictions, poverty, illness. Like an expert physician or a skilled and kind nurse, He tries to cure a sick man from dangerous spiritual illnesses. If a servant is blessed by God, he will be faced with afflictions until he turns his attention to God the Almighty, and is refined. This is the way, and other than this there is no way, but man must tread this path with his own feet until he reaches its conclusion. If he does not reach any conclusion in this way, and the misled man is not cured, and he does not deserve the blessings of heaven, when his soul is drawn from him there will be much pressure on him, so perhaps he will return and be aware. Again, if he is not affected, then in the grave, in the world of *barzakh*, and in the terrible perilous events which take place after death, he will suffer pressures and chastisement until he becomes purified and refined, and he will not go to hell. All of these are blessings from Almighty God to prevent man from going to hell. What then if with all these blessings and favors from Almighty God he is still not cured? Then there is no other alternative but the last cure, which is that he should be burned. How many a man has not refined and reformed himself and was not affected by these cures, so that he needed God, the Merciful, the Compassionate, to refine His servant by fire, just as gold must be purified in fire.

Regarding the *ayah* (verse): *"Living therein for ages,"* (78:23), it has been reported that the 'ages' mentioned here are for those who have been guided, those the basis of whose faith has been preserved.[21] This is for me and you, if we are believers. Each age lasts for thousands of years, how many, God only knows. God forbid that we reach such a state

---

[21] 'Ayashi narrates from Humran who asked from Imam Baqir, Peace be with him, about the *ayah* mentioned, and he answered: "This is about those who will depart from the fire." *Majma' al-Bayan*, Vol. 10, p. 424.

that these cures are not effective, so that for deserving and meriting the everlasting blessings [of heaven] this final cure is required. God forbid that it should be necessary that a man should go to hell for a while and burn there until he is purified from his vices, spiritual pollution and filthy Satanic attributes, so that he may become deserving and capable of benefiting from *"gardens beneath which rivers flow."* (58:22) Beware that this is only for those whose sins have not reached such an extent that they are entirely deprived of the mercy and blessings of God the Almighty, those who yet have an essential merit for going to heaven. God forbid that a man, due to the multitude of his sins he should be expelled and blocked from the presence of God the Almighty, and that he should be bereft of the divine mercy, so that there is no other way for him but to remain forever in the fire of hell. God forbid that you should be bereft of divine mercy and blessings, and that you should be subject to His wrath, anger and chastisements. May your deeds, behavior and speech not be themeans to the denial of grace, so that there is no way for you but eternal damnation.

Now, while you cannot bear to keep a hot stone in your hand for a minute, keep the fire of hell away! Keep these fires from the seminaries and from the clerical community. Keep disputes and strife far from your hearts. Behave well with people, and in company, and be compassionate and kind. Of course, you are not to be nice to sinners with regard to their sins and rebelliousness. Tell him to his face of his ugly deeds and wrongdoing, and prohibit him from it; and keep yourselves from promoting anarchy and from rebellion. Behave well with the servants of God and the righteous. Show respect to the learned with regard to their knowledge, to those on the path of guidance with regard to their virtue, and to the ignorant and unlearned, for they are also the servants of God. Have good behavior, be kind, honest and brotherly. Refine yourselves. You want to refine and guide the community, but how can one who is not able to reform and manage himself guide and manage others? Now there are only a few days left in the month of *Sha'ban*, so try in these few days to repent and reform yourselves, and enter the blessed month of *Ramadan* with a healthy soul.

Points Regarding Munajat of the Month of Sha'ban

Have you said the *Munajat* of *Sha'ban* for God, the Blessed and Supreme, during this month of *Sha'ban* in which it has been advised to recite this devotion from the first until the last of the month? Have you benefited from its lofty meanings which teach increased faith and knowledge (*ma'arifat*) with regard to the station of the Lord? It is reported with regard to this supplication that it is the *munajat* of Imam Ali, Peace be with him, and his descendants, and that all of the immaculate Imams, Peace be with them, called upon Allah by this devotion.[22] Very few supplications and devotions (*du'a wa munajat*) may be found which were recited by all of the Imams (AS) for God. This devotion is truly an introduction to admonish and prepare man to accept the responsibilities of the blessed month of *Ramadan*, and it is possible that it

---

[22] Cf. *Iqbal al-A'mal*, Works for the Month of Sha'ban, p. 685; and *Misbah al-Mutahajjid wa Salah al-Muta'bah*, p. 374; and *Bihar al-Anwar*, Vol. 91, p. 97-99, "*The Book of Dhikr ad Du'a*", Chapter 32, Hadith 12.

is also to remind the aware person of the motive for fasting and its valuable fruits.

The immaculate Imams, Peace be with them, have explained many things by the tongue of supplication. The tongue of supplication is very different from the other tongues by which those greats explained precepts. They have explained most spiritual, metaphysical, and precisely divine matters, and that which is related to knowledge of Allah by the tongue of supplication. But we recite supplications to the end and unfortunately pay no attention to their meanings, and we fail to understand what they really want to say.

In this *munajat* we read: "O my God! Grant that I may be perfectly cut off from all else but You, and enlighten the vision of our hearts by the radiance of vision toward You, until the visions of the heart tear through the curtains of light and attach to the Source of Greatness and our souls come to belong to Your Exalted Sanctity."[23]

---

[23] *Bihar al-Anwar*, vol. 19, part 2, old edition, "*bab al- ad'iyyah wa al- munzajat*," pp. 89-90.

It is possible that the meaning of the sentence, "O my God! Grant that I may be perfectly cut off from all else but You," is that prior to the blessed month of *Ramadan*, divinely aware people should get ready and prepare themselves for cutting themselves off and avoiding worldly pleasures (and this avoidance is that very being cut off perfectly from all else but Allah). Being perfectly cut off from all else is not something easily obtained. It requires extra hard practice, going to some lengths, spiritual exercises, perseverance, and discipline, until one is able to fix one's attention completely on nothing but God and cut himself off from all else.

If someone is able to do this, he has reached a great felicity. However, with the least attention to this world it is impossible to be cut off from all else but Allah. Someone who wants to perform the fast of the blessed month of *Ramadan* with such manners as he has been asked to, must cut himself off completely from all else so that he can observe the manners for the celebration and feast [of Allah], coming to know of the station of the Host, insofar as this is possible.

According to the order of the Holy Apostle, Peace be upon him and with his progeny, (which is related in one of his sermons) all of the servants of God, the Supreme, have been invited by Him to a feast in the blessed month of *Ramadan* and are to be the guests of the Provider at His feast. He says there: "O you people! The month of Allah is approaching you ... and you have been invited in it to the feast of Allah."[24] In these few days until the blessed monthof *Ramadan*, you should reflect, reform yourselves, and pay attention to God the Almighty, seek forgiveness for your unbecoming behavior and deeds, and if, God forbid, you have committed a sin, repent for it prior to entering the blessed month of *Ramadan*. Habituate your tongue to intimate devotions (*munajat*) to God the Almighty.

God forbid that in the blessed month of *Ramadan* you should backbite or slander, or in short, sin, and so become polluted by transgression inthe presence of the Lord, the Exalted, at His feast. You have been invited

---

[24] From *Wasa'il al-Shi'ah*, Vol. 7, p. 227, 'The Book of Fasting, Chapter on the Month of *Ramadan*' Ch. 18, hadith 20.

during this honorable month to the banquet of God the Almighty, "and you have been invited in it to the feast of Allah," so, get yourself ready for the magnificent feast of the Almighty. At least respect the formal and exoteric manners of fasting. (The true manners of fasting are another matter entirely, and require constant care and effort.) The meaning of fasting is not merely refraining from eating and drinking, one must also keep oneself from sin. This is the primary etiquette of fasting for novices. (The etiquette of fasting for divine people who want to reach the mine of greatness is other than this.) You should at least observe the primary etiquette of fasting, and in the same way that you refrain from eating and drinking, you should keep your eyes, ears and tongue from transgression. From now on, keep your tongue from backbiting, slander, speaking bad, and lies, and expel from your hearts all spite, envy, and other ugly Satanic attributes. If you are able, cut yourself off from all but Allah. Perform your deeds sincerely and without duplicity. Cut yourselves offfrom the Satans among humans and the jinn, although we ourselves apparently cannot aspire to reaching such a valuable state of felicity. At least try to see to it that your fast is not accompanied by sin. Otherwise, even if your fast is correct from the point of view of Islamic law, it will ascend to be accepted by God.

There is a big difference between the ascension of one's works and their acceptance on the one hand and their religious correctness on the other. If, by the end of the blessed month of *Ramadan*, there is no change in your works and deeds, and your ways and manners are no different than they were before the month of fasting, it is evident that the fast which you were expected to perform was not realized; and that which you have done is no more than a vulgar physical fast.

In this noble month, in which you have been invited to the divine banquet, if you do not gain insight (*ma'rifat*) about God the Almighty nor insight into yourself, it means that you have not properly participated in the feast of Allah. You must not forget that in this blessed month, which is the 'month of

Allah', in which the way of divine mercy is opened to the servants of God and the satans and devils, according to some reports, are locked in chains,[25] if you are not able to reform and refine yourselves, and to manage and control your *nafs-e amarah* (the commanding self),[26] to subdue your selfish lusts and to cut off your relations and interests with this world and material things, then after the end of the month of fasting it will be difficult for you to be able to accomplish this. Therefore, take advantage of this opportunity before the magnificent grace of it vanishes, and purify and reform yourselves. Get ready and prepare to perform the duties of the month of fasting. Let it not be that prior to the arrival of the month of *Ramadan* you are like one who is wound up by the hand of Satan so that in this single

---

[25] It is reported from Jabar that Abu Ja'far, Imam Baqir, Peace be with him, said: The Prophet of Allah turned his face toward the people and said: O company of people! When the crescent moon of the month of *Ramadan* appears, the rebellious Satans are locked up, and the doors of heaven, the doors of paradise and the doors of mercy are opened, and the doors to the Fire are shut, and prayers are answered. From *Wasa'il alShi'ah*, Vol. 7, p. 224, "The Book of Fasting", "The Section on the Precepts of the Fast of the Month of *Ramadan*", section 18, hadith 14.

[26] The 'commanding self' is an expression used in the Qur'an, associated with one's base desires, cf. 12:53. [Tr.]

month when the satans are enchained you automatically busy yourselves with sin and deeds opposed to the orders of Islam! Sometimes due to his distancefrom God and the great number of his sins, the rebellious and sinful man sinks so low into darkness and ignorance that he does not need Satan to tempt him, but he himself takes on the color of Satan. *"Sibghat Allah"*[27] *is* the opposite of the color of Satan.

Someone who pursues selfish desires and who is obedient to Satan, gradually turns the color of Satan. You should decide at least in this one month to control yourselves, and to avoid speech and behavior which displeases God, the Supreme. Right now in this very session make a covenant with God that during the blessed month of *Ramadan* that you will avoid backbiting, slander and speaking ill of others. Bring your tongue, eyes, hands, ears and other organs and limbs under your control. Manage your deeds and your words. It is possible that this same worthy deed will result in God's paying

---

[27] *"Sibghat Allah,"* The color of Allah, cf. (2:138), is the opposite of the "color of Satan". [Tr.]

attention to you and blessing you. After the month of fasting, when the satans are released from their chains, you will have been reformed, and you will no longer listen to the lies of Satan, and you will refine yourselves. I repeat, decide during these thirty days of the blessed month of *Ramadan* to control your tongue, eyes, ears and all your organs and limbs, and pay constant attention to the judgement of the *shari'ah* about the works you intend to do, and the words you intend to speak and the subject you intend to listen to. This is the elementary and outward manner of keeping a fast. At least keep to this outward manner of fasting! If you observe that someone is about to backbite, prevent him and say to him that we have made a covenant that during these thirty days of *Ramadan* to keep ourselves from prohibited affairs. And if you are not able to keep him from backbiting, leave that session. Do not just sit there and listen. The Muslims must be safe from you. Someone from whose hands, tongue and eyes other Muslims are not safe is not truly a Muslim,[28] although he may be outwardly and formally a Muslim who has formally proclaimed: *"La illaha illa Allah"* (There is nogod but Allah). If, God forbid, you want to offend somebody, to slander them or to backbite, you should know that you are in the presence of the Lord; you are to be the guest of God the Almighty, and in the presence of God, the Supreme, you would behave rudely to one of His servants; and to slander one of the servants of God is to slander God. They are the servants of God; especially if they are scholars on the path of knowledge and piety (*taqwa*). Sometimes you see that because of such affairs man reaches such a state that he denies God at the moment of his death! He denies the divine signs: *"Then evil was the end of those who did evil, because they rejected the signs of Allah and used to mock them."* (30:10) These things occur gradually. Today, an incorrect

---

[28] Abu Ja'far [Imam Baqir], Peace be with him, said that the Apostle of Allah, may the Peace and Blessings of Allah be with him and with his progeny, said: "Shall I tell you of the believer? The believer is one whom the believers trust with their lives and their property. Shall I tell you of the Muslim? The Muslim is one from whose tongue and the Muslims are safe." From *Usul al-Kafi*, Vol. 3, p. 331, "The Book of Faith and Infidelity", "Chapter of the Believer, His signs and attributes", hadith 19.

view; tomorrow, a word of backbiting; and the next day, slander against a Muslim, and little by little these sins accumulate in the heart, and make the heart black and prevent man from attaining knowledge (*ma'arifat*) of Allah, until it reaches the point that he denies everything and rejects the truth.

According to some *ayat* of the Qur'an as interpreted through some reports, the deeds of men will be presented to the Prophet (S) and the pure Imam's (AS) and will be reviewed by them.[29] When the Prophet reviews your deeds and he sees how many errors and sins there are, how upset and distressed will he be? You do not want the Apostle of God to become upset and distressed; you would not want to break his heart and make him sad. When he witnesses that the page of your

---

[29] For example, "And say: Work, so Allah will see your work and (so will) His Apostle and the believers: and you shall be brought back to the Knower of the unseen and the seen, then He will inform you of what you did." (9:105) Also, Abu Basir reported that Imam Sadiq (AS) said: The deeds will be reviewed by the Apostle of Allah, Peace be with him and with his progeny, the deeds of the servants, each morning, the good ones and the bad ones, so be careful. This is what Allah the Supreme said: "Work, so Allah will see your work and (so will) His Apostle". *Usul Kafi*, Vol. 1, p. 318, The Book of Hujjah, Chapter on the Presentation of the deeds to the Apostle and the Imams, Peace be with them. Hadith 1,2-6. *Tafsir Burhan*, Vol. 2, p. 157.

deeds is replete with backbiting, slander, and speaking ill of other Muslims and that all your attention was devoted to this worldly and materialistic affairs and that your heart was overflowing with malice, hatred, spite and suspicion towards each other, it is possible that in the presence of God, the Supreme and Holy, and the angels of Allah, he will be embarrassed that his community and followers were ungrateful for their divine blessings, and thus unbridled and heedless they betrayed the trust of God, the Holy and Supreme. Someone who is related to us, even if in a menial position, if he errs, we become embarrassed. You are related to the Apostle of Allah, may the Peace and Blessings of Allah be with him and with his progeny; by entering the seminary, you have related yourself to the Law of Islam, the most Noble Apostle and the Noble Qur'an. If you perform ugly deeds, it upsets the Prophet and he cannot bear it, and God forbid, you may be damned. Do not let the Apostle of Allah, Peace be upon him and his with progeny, and the pure Imams become upset and saddened. The heart of man is like a mirror, clear and bright, and because of too much attention to this world and too many sins, it becomes dark. However, if a person at least performs the fast for God the Almighty sincerely and without duplicity (I am not saying that other acts of worship are not to be pure; it is necessary for all of the acts of worship to be performed sincerely and without duplicity), then this worship which is a turning away from lust, putting aside pleasure, and cutting oneself off from all but God, if it is performed well in this single month, perhaps the grace of God will be extended to him and the mirror of his heart will be cleaned of its blackness and tarnish; and there is hope that he will change his ways and become dissuaded from this wilderness and worldly pleasures. When the Night of Power[30] arrives, one will gain the illumination which is obtained on that night by the friends of God and the believers.

The reward of such a fast is God, as it has been reported: The fast is for Me and I am its

---

[30] The Night of Power is a night near the end of *Ramadan* in which the Qur'an was revealed to the Prophet (PBUH) and which, according to the Qur'an is a night better than one thousand months. Cf. Qur'an, *Surah Qadr* (97). [Tr.]

reward."[31] Nothing else could be the reward of such a fast. A garden of blessings would not count as a worthy reward for sucha fast. If a man takes fasting to mean closing his mouth to food but opening it for backbiting, and in the warm and friendly meetings with company in the nights when there is opportunity and time he engages in backbiting until *sahar*,[32] such fasting will be of no benefit and have no effect. Rather, one who fasts in this way has not observed the etiquette of the banquet of God. He has violated the rights of his Benefactor, the Benefactor Who has provided him with all the means and conveniences of life before creating him, and has provided for the means of his development. He sent the prophets to guide him. He sent down the heavenly books. Man has been given the power to approach the source of greatness and the light of felicity, has been favored with intellect and perception, and has been the recipient of His generosity. Now, He has invited His servants

---

[31] *Furu' al-Kafi*, Vol. 4, p. 63, "The Book of Fasting", "The Chapter of the Grace of the Fast and the one who keeps the fast", hadith 6.

[32] *Sahar* is the period from the first light of the morning until sunrise. [Tr.]

to enter His guest house and to sit at the table of His blessings where they are to thank and to praise Him to the extent that their tongues and hands are able. Is it right for the servants who benefit at the table of His blessings and who use the means and conveniences which He has freely provided for them that they should oppose their Master and Host and to rebel against Him? Is it right that they should use these things in opposition to Him and against His wishes? Wouldn't this be biting the hand that feeds one and the height of ingratitude for man to sit at the table of his Master and with rude and impudent behavior and actions to audaciously insult his honored Host Who is his benefactor, performing ugly and evil deeds before the Host?

The guests must at least know Who their Host is, and become aware of His dignity. They should be acquainted with the customs and manners of the sessions. They should try not to rebel by performing deeds which conflict with virtue and decorum. The guests of the Supreme Being must come to know the divine station of the presence of the Lord of Majesty —a station of which the Imams, Peace be with them, and the great divine prophets were constantly seeking greater knowledge and more perfect awareness, and wanted to obtain such a source of light and greatness. "And enlighten the eyes of our hearts with the light of the radiance of looking at You, until the vision of the hearts tears through the curtains of light and is then united with the source of greatness." The banquet of Allah is that very "source of greatness". God, the Blessed and Exalted, has invited His servants to enter the source of light and greatness. However, if the servant is not appropriate, he will not be able to enter into such a splendid and sumptuous position. God, the Exalted, has invited his servants to all sorts of favors and boons and to numerous spiritual pleasures, but if they are not prepared to be present at such lofty positions, they will not be able to enter. How can one enter the presence of the Lord and the guest house of the Lord of lords which is the source of greatness with spiritual pollution, vices, and sins of the body and soul?

It requires merit. Preparation is necessary. In disgrace and with polluted hearts which are covered by veils of darkness, one will not be able to understand these spiritual meanings and truths. One must tear these veils and push aside these dark and light curtains which cover the heart and are barriers to union with Allah so that one will be able to enter the brilliant and splendid divine company.

The Veils of Man

Attention to other than God covers man with veils of darkness and light. If any worldly affair is a cause for man's attention to be directed toward the world and to neglect God, the Exalted, it raises dark veils. All of the corporeal worlds are dark veils. If the world is a means of directing attention to the Truth and for arriving at the abode of the Hereafter, which is the '"abode of honor", then the dark veils are transformed into veils of light. "Being perfectly cut off from all else" means tearing and pushing aside all the dark and light veils, until one is able to enter the divine guest house which is the "source of greatness". Hence, in this intimate devotion (*munajat*) there is a request to God, the Exalted, for vision and brightness of the heart so one may tear the veils of light and reach the source of greatness: "Until the vision of the heart tears through the veils of light, so that there is union with the source of greatness."

However, one who has not yet torn the veils of darkness, one who directs all of his attention to the natural world and, God forbid, becomes deviated from Allah, and one who is basically unaware of the world beyond and the spiritual worlds, and has retrogressed to a state of nature, who has never decided to refine himself, to set into motion his spiritual powers, to push aside the curtains of darkness which are a cloud over his heart, he is lodged in 'the deepest of the depths' [of hell] which is the ultimate veil: *"Then we render him the lowest of the low."* (95:5), while the God of the worlds has created man in the most lofty state and station: *"Indeed We have created man in the best of molds."* (95:4). If one follows the desires of the self and from the day he becomes acquainted with himself pays no attention to anything other than the dark wilderness[33] and never thinks that it is possible that aside from this polluted dark world that there exists another place and station, then he will have sunk into the veil of darkness and have become an instance of: *"but he clung to the earth and followed his low desire."* (7:176).

---

[33] Imam uses the expression *"'alam zulumani tabi'at"*, literally the dark world of nature, but here, by nature is not meant all things natural, as opposed to artificial, but unrefined and base. [Tr.]

With such a heart polluted by sin that he has been covered by the curtain of darkness, and with such a gloomy spirit that due to the effect of numerous sins he has become far from God, the Exalted, that worship of desire and seeking after the world have blinded the intellect and eyes of truth, then he cannot be released from the veils of darkness, let alone to tear the veils of light and detach himself from all but Allah. The strongestsort of belief he might have would be not to deny the position of the saints (*awliya*) of God, and not to consider as myths the worlds of the *barzakh*, the *sirat*, the resurrection, the accounting, the book, heaven and hell. Due to the effects of sins and the attachment of the heart to this world, one comes to gradually deny these truths, to deny the positions of the saints (*awliya*) of God, positions which are mentioned in not more than a few lines of prayers and intimate devotions.

Knowledge and Faith

Sometimes you see that one has knowledge of these realities but has no faith. Undertakers are not afraid of the dead, for they have certainty that the dead cannot harm one, even when he was alive and had a spirit in his body he was not harmful, so what harm can he be now as an empty frame? However, those who are afraid of the dead are afraid because they do not have faith in this truth. They merely have knowledge. They know about God and the Day of Atonement, but they lack certainty. The heart is unaware of that which the intellect has understood. They know the proofs for the existence of God and the reality of the Resurrection, but these very same intellectual proofs may be veils covering the heart which do not permit the light of faith to shine in. Until God, the Exalted, frees them from the darknesses and obscurities and leads them to enter the worlds of light and radiances: *"Allah is the Guardian (Wali) of those who believe; He brings them out of the darknesses into the light."* (2:257) He whose Guardian (*Wali*) is God, the Blessed and Exalted, and who is taken by Him out from the darknesses never commits another sin, never backbites, never slanders others, and he is never vengeful or envious of his brothers in faith. His own heart is filled with a feeling of luminosity and he no longer holds the world or what it contains in high esteem. As Imam 'Ali (AS) said: "If all the world and what it contains were offered to me to cruelly and unjustly take the skin of a grain of barley from the mouth of an ant, I would never accept it."[34]

But some of you trample over everything, and you backbite the great [scholars] of Islam. If others speak ill of the grocers and perfume sellers on the street and backbite them, for your part some of you relate unfair things, insult and are impudent toward the scholars of Islam, becauseyou are not firmly grounded in faith and you do not believe in [divine] retribution for your own deeds. Impeccability ('ismat) is nothing but perfect faith. The meaning of the impeccability of the prophets and the Friends of God ('awliya)

---

[34] "By Allah, if the seven climes and what is under their skies were offered to me to be sinful to Allah by taking the skin of a grain of barley from an ant, I would not do it."*Nahj al-Balagha*, Sermon 215.

is not that, for instance, Gabriel took them by the hand. Of course, if Gabriel had taken the hand of Shimr,[35] he would never have committed a sin. However, impeccability is the offspring of faith. If a man had faith in God, the Exalted, and if he saw God Almighty with the eyes of his heart as one sees the sun, it would not be possible for him to commit a sin, just as if he were standing before an armed power, he would find some 'impeccability'. This fear comes from belief in the [divine] presence, which keeps man from committing sin. The Impeccable (*ma'sumin*), Peace be with them, after their creation from pure clay, because of the effects of their spiritual discipline, and acquisition of radiance and virtuous character traits, always see themselves as being in the presence of God, Who knows all things and encompasses all affairs. They have faith in the meaning of the words, *"La illaha illa Allah"* (There is no god but Allah), and they believe that other than God, all persons and all things are perishing and have no role in

---

[35] Shimr was the assassin of Imam Husayn, Peace be with him, and symbolizes evil. [Tr.]

determining man's destiny: *"All things are perishing but His Face."* (28:88)

If man is certain and has faith that all the outward and inward worlds are in the presence of the Lord, and that God, the Exalted is present everywhere and sees everything, in the presence of God and God's blessings there would be no possibility for committing sins. Man is not able to commit sins before a discerning child, and he does not expose his private parts, so how could he expose his private parts before God, the Exalted, and not dread to commit a crime? This is because he has faith in the presence of the child, however, with regard to the divine presence, if he has knowledge, he still lacks faith. Due to the multiplicity of his sins which have darkened and blackened his heart, he is totally unable to accept such truths, and may not even consider them to be likely.

Actually, man would not recklessly run wild if he considered it at all likely—he need not have certainty—that which is reported in the Noble Qur'an is right, the promises and the threats, and that he should amend his ways and deeds. If you consider it at all likely that ferocious beasts are to be found along the path which might harm you, or that there are armed bandits who might hold you up, you would refrain from taking that path, and you would try to ascertain the correctness or incorrectness of these reports. Is it possible for someone to consider it possible that hell exists and that one may remain forever in its fire while at the same time doing wrong?

Can it be said that one who considers God the Almighty to be present and watching and Who sees himself to be in the presence of the Lord, and who considers it possible that there should be retribution for his words and deeds, a reckoning and chastisement, and that in this world every word he speaks, every step he takes, every deed he does, is recorded by angels of Allah called 'Raqib' and 'Atid',[36] and they carefully record all his words and deeds, and in such a state, could he be fearless of his own wrongdoing? It is painful [to realize] that they do not even

---

[36] "He utters not a word but there is by him a watcher at hand (raqibun 'atidun)." (50:18)

consider these truths to be possible. From the manners of some and theirway of living it is obvious that they do not even consider the existence of a supernatural world to be possible, since the mere consideration of this possibility keeps man from committing many wrongs.

The First Step in Refinement

How long do you wish to remain in the sleep of negligence, plunged in corruption? Fear God! Beware of the aftermath of your deeds! Wake up from the sleep of negligence! You have not yet awakened. You have not yet taken the first step. The first step of wayfaring is *yaqzah* (awakening),but you are still asleep. Your eyes may be open, but your hearts are asleep. If your hearts were not so sleepy and rusted and blackened with the effects of sin, you would not continue your wrongful deeds and words so carelessly and indifferently. If you thought a bit about the affairs of the other world and its terrible path you would give more importance to the heavy duties and responsibilities which rest upon your shoulders.

There is also another world for you, there is also the resurrection. (You are not like other existents for which there is no returning.) Why do you not take warning? Why are you not awake and conscious? Why do you so heedlessly engage in backbiting and speaking ill of your Muslim brothers, or listening to such things? Do you not know that the tongue which wags in backbiting will be trampled under the feet of others on the day of the resurrection? Have you heard that backbiting will be food for the dogs of hell?[37] Have you never given a thought to how evil are the consequences of these differences, enmities, jealousies, cynicism and selfishness, and arrogance and conceit? Do you know that the repercussion of these wicked forbidden deeds is hell and that it is possible, God forbid, that they will lead to the everlasting fire?

God does not want man to be afflicted with illnesses unaccompaniedby pain, for when an illness is accompanied by pain, it forces man to seeka cure, to consult a doctor or go to a hospital, but an unfelt illness without pain is more dangerous. By the time one becomes aware of it, it is too late. If mental illnesses were accompanied by pain, this

---

[37] In the advice given by the Commander of the Faithful (Imam Ali (AS)) to Nuf al-Bakali it is stated: "Keep away from backbiting, for it will be food for the dogs of hell."*Wasa'il al-Shi'ah*, Vol. 8, p. 600, the Book of Hajj, the Chapters on the Precepts of the Ten, Ch. 152, hadith 16.

would be something for which to be thankful. Ultimately, man would be forced to find a cure or a remedy. But what can be done about such dangerous diseases for which there is no pain? The illnesses of arrogance and selfishness are without pain. Other sins corrupt the heart and the spirit without causing any pain. Not only are these illnesses unaccompanied by pain, but they also bring apparent pleasure. Meetings and sessions of backbiting are very warm and sweet! Love of the self and love of the world, which are the roots of all sins, are pleasurable.[38] One who is afflicted with dropsy may die from water, but yet enjoy drinking it untilhis last breath.[39]

Naturally, if one gets pleasure from an illness, and it also has no pain, he will not

---

[38] It is reported that Abi Abdillah (Imam Ja'far), Peace be with him, said: The head of all sins is love of the world. *Usul al-Kafi*, Vol. 4, p. 2, The Book of Faith and Infidelity, The Chapter on Love of the World and Avarice toward it, hadith 1. *Usul al-Kafi*, Vol. 3, p. 197, The Book of Faith and Infidelity, The Chapter on Derogation of the World and Asceticism in it, hadith 11. *Bihar al-Anwar*, Vol. 70, p. 1; and Vol. 74, p. 178.

[39] One of the symptoms of dropsy is inordinate thirst. In Arabic the disease is called *istisqa'* and one who has the disease is *mustasqa*. [Tr.]

seek any cure for it. However much he is warned that it is fatal, he will not believe it. If someone is afflicted with the illnesses of hedonism and worshipping the world, and his heart is filled with love ofthe world, he will grow weary of all else but the world and what is in it. Allah forbid, he will be become an enemy of God, the servants of God, the divine prophets and *'awliya*, and the angels of Allah. He will have a sense of hatred and loathing for them, and when the angels come at the command of the Glorious God to take his soul, he will have a feeling of repulsion and abhorrence, for he will see that God and the angels of Allah want to separate him from his beloved (the world and worldly things).

It is possible that he will leave the world with hostility and enmity toward the Presence of the Exalted Truth (God). One of the great men of Qazvin, may Allah have mercy on him, reported that he was present at the bedside of someone at the moment of his death. During the last instants of his life, he opened his eyes and said: "The oppression with which God has afflicted me, no one has ever afflicted! Now, God wants to separate me from these children whom I have taken such pains to raise. Is there any greater oppression than this?" If one has not refined oneself, and has not averted oneself from the world, and has not expelled love of the world from his heart, there is the fear that he will die with a heart overflowing with anger and hatred toward God and His 'awliya. He will have to contend with an ominous destiny. Is such an unbridled man to be considered as the crown of creation or as the most vile of creatures? "By Time. Surely man is lost, except for he who believes and does good works, and enjoin upon each other truth, and enjoin upon each other patience." In this *surah*, the only exceptions are the believers who perform good works. And a good work is a work which is congruous with the spirit. However, you see that many of man's works are only congruent with the body. "Enjoining is also not practiced. If you are dominated by love of the world and love of the self, and if this prevents you from perceiving truths and realities, and prevents you from performing deeds purely for God, and if you are kept from enjoining the truth and enjoining patience, and you are thereby obstructed from the way to guidance, then you will be lost. You will be lost in this world and in the next, for you will have given up your youth and will be prohibited from the blessings of heaven and otherworldly advantages, and also lack this world. If others have no way to heaven, and if the doors to divine mercy are closed to them, if they are to abide eternally in the fire of hell, at least they will have had the world, they will have enjoyed worldly advantages, but you ...

Beware, lest love of the world and love of the self gradually increase within you, to the point that Satan is able to take away your faith. It is said that all of the efforts of Satan are for the sake of robbing faith.[40] All of his efforts and labors, night and day, are for the sake of taking away the faith of men. No one has given you a document to guarantee your faith. Perhaps one's faith is merely on loan

---

[40] "He [Iblis] said: As You have caused me to remain disappointed, I will certainly lie in wait for them in Your straight path." (7:16) In the exegesis of Ali ibn Ibrahim pertaining to this ayah it is written: "If people tread the path of guidance, Satan tries to make them leave the path of religion." *Tafsir* of Ali ibn Ibrahim, Vol. 1 , p. 224; *Tafsir Burhan*, Vol. 2, p. 5.

(*mustawda'*),[41] and in the end Satan will get it, and you will leave this world with enmity for the Blessed and Exalted God and His *'awliya*. Perhaps one will have enjoyed an entire life of divine blessings, provided for by Imam Zaman (AS),[42] and, God forbid, in the end one may give up his life without faith and in enmity toward the Bestower of the Blessings.

If you have any interest in, relation with and affection for the world, try to cut it. This world, with all its superficial splendor and glitter is too insignificant to be worthy of love, especially for one who has divested himself of such superficialities of life. What do you have of this world that your heart

---

[41] In a narration from the family of the Prophet (AS) under *ayah* 98, *Surah alAn'am*, pertaining to the phrase, "a resting place and a depository", it is said that the faiths of individuals may be divided into two kinds, fixed and borrowed. As in the narration from Muhammad ibn al-Fudayl from Musa ibn al-Ja'far (AS) who said: "Faith which is in a resting place will be fixed until the day of the resurrection. Faith which is in a depository will be taken by God prior to death." *Tafsir 'Ayashi*, Vol. 1, p. 401. In *Nahj al-Balagha* it is also to be found that: "A kind of faith is fixed in the heart, and another kind is loaned in the hearts and breasts until the time of death." *Nahj al-Balagha*, Sermon 231.

[42] The phrase used is more literally, "sitting at the table of Imam Zaman (AS)", indicating that the religious students are provided for through religious donations. [Tr.]

should be attached to it? You have nought but the mosque, the prayer niche, the seminary, the corner of a room. Is it proper for you to compete for the mosque and the prayer niche?

Should this be a cause of disagreement among you, to corrupt the society? Suppose that, like the worldly people, you had a comfortable sumptuous life, and that, God forbid, you spent your life on feasting and drinking. After your life is over, you would see that your life had passed like a pleasant dream, but the requital and liability for it will be with you always. What value does this fleeting and apparently sweet life have (assuming that it is very sweet) in comparison to endless chastisement? The chastisement of worldly people is sometimes endless. The worldly people who imagine that they have acquired the world and benefit from its advantages and boons, are remiss and mistaken. Everyone sees the world from the window of his own environment and situation, and imagines that the world is exactly that which he has. The physical world is broader than that which man imagines he has acquired, discovered and through which he roams. It has been narrated about this world with all its means and ways that: "He has never looked kindly upon it."[43] So, how must the other world be upon which God, the Blessed and Exalted, has looked kindly? What is the source of greatness to which man is called and what is it like? Man is too low to comprehend the source of greatness.

If you purify your intentions, rectify your deeds, expel love of self and position from your hearts, a high station will be prepared for you. The whole world and what exists in it along with its superficial aspects is not worth even a cent by comparison to the station prepared for the righteous servants of God. Try to achieve this lofty station. If you are able, try to make something of yourselves and improve yourselves so that you may pay no heed even to this lofty

---

[43] The full text of the hadith is: "For God, the Glorious and Exalted, the world is without value; and among the creatures known to us which God has created, there is no existent more despicable to Him than the world, and since the time when He created the world, God has never looked kindly upon it." *Bihar al-Anwar*, Vol. 70, p. 110, The Book of Faith and Infidelity, Ch. 122, hadith 109.

station. Do not worship God in order to reach this station, but rather call upon Him and prostrate yourselves with your heads upon the earth before Him because He is worthy of worship and the Almighty.[44] In that case you will have torn through the curtains of light and have attained the source of greatness. Can you obtain such a position with these deeds and actions which you perform?Can this be reached by the path you tread? Is it easy to be saved from divine chastisement and to escape the terrible torment and the fire of hell? Do you imagine that the weeping of the Pure Imams and the cries of Imam Sajjad (AS) were a teaching, and that they wanted to instruct others about how to cry? With all this spirituality and the lofty position they hold, they wept for fear of God! They understood how difficult and dangerous it is to advance along the way

---

[44] It is narrated from Imam Sadiq (AS): Worship is of three kinds: one group worships God from fear, this is the worship of the servants; another group worships God in order to obtain a reward, this is the worship of hirelings; and the third group worships God, the Great and Lofty, because of love, and this is the worship of the free. And this is the most excellent worship." *Wasa'il al-Shi'a*, Vol. 1, p. 45, The Chapters of Introduction to Worship, Ch. 9, hadith 1. *Usul al-Kafi*, Vol. III, p. 131, the Book of Faith and Infidelity, Ch. on worship, hadith 5.

before them. They were aware of the difficulties, hardships and problems of crossing the *sirat*, which has this world at one end and the next world at the other and which passes through hell. They were aware of the worlds of the grave, of the *barzakh*,and of the resurrection, and of their terrible torments, and hence theywere never content and always took refuge in God from the intense chastisements of the other world.

What thought have you given to these terrible devastating torments, and what way have you found to salvation from them? When are you going to decide to reform and refine yourselves? Now, while you are young, and have the strength of youth, and you have power over your faculties, and physical weakness has not yet overtaken you, if you do not think of refinement and of making something of yourselves, then how will you be able to do it when you become old, when your bodies and souls are in the grip of weakness and feebleness, and you have lost your will power, your decisiveness and your resistance, and when the burden of your sins has blackened your hearts? With every breath and every step you take, and with each passing moment of your life, reform becomes more difficult, and it is possible for darkness and corruption to increase. The more one's age advances, the more the things which conflict with human felicity multiply and the more one's powers are weakened. Thus, when old age arrives, it is difficult to be successful at refinement and the acquisition of the virtues and piety (*taqwa*). One is unable to repent, for repentance is not merely the verbal expression, "I repent before Allah", rather, contrition and the resolve to abandon one's sin are also necessary.[45] Such contrition and resolve are not to be obtained by one who has engaged in backbiting and lying for fifty or seventy years, whose beard has become white with sin and transgression. Such a person is afflicted with sin to the end of his life.

---

[45] It is narrated that Imam Ali (AS) said: "Verily, asking for forgiveness is a degree of the *'Illiyyin* and it is a word that means six things. The first of them is regret for what has occurred. The second is resolve not to return to that evil ever again... " *Nahj al-Balagha*, p.1281, *Hikmat* 409. For more information refer to *Forty Hadiths*: An Exposition by Imam Khomeini, hadith 17, translated by Ali Qara'i in the journal, *Al-Tawhid*, Vol. VII, No. 2, pp. 39-52. Note that the *'Illiyyin* are those of the most lofty heights of heaven. Cf. Qur'an (83:17). [Tr.]

Youths should not sit still until the dust of age turns them grey. (I have reached old age, and am aware of its misfortunes and difficulties.) While you are young, you are able to accomplish something. While you enjoy the strength and determination of youth you can expel selfish desires, worldly attractions and animal wants from yourselves. However, if you do not think about reform and making something of yourselves while you are young, it will be too late when you become old. Think, while you are young, before you become old and exhausted. A young heart is subtle and celestial, and within it the motivation for corruption is weak. However, the older one gets the stronger and more firm is the source of sin implanted in the heart, until it can no longer be uprooted, as it is reported: The heart of man is clear and shining like a mirror. With each sin a man commits, another black mark is added to the heart, until it becomes black, so that it is possible that a night and day cannot pass without the commission of a sin against the Lord.[46]

When old age arrives, it is difficult to return ones heart to its original form and state. If, God forbid, you have not reformed yourself when you leave the world, in what manner do you expect to meet God, when y our heart is black and your eyes, ears and tongue are polluted by sins? How can you return that with which you have been entrusted by God when it has become polluted and wicked, while it was given to you in perfect purity and cleanliness? These eyes and ears which are under your control, this hand and tongue which are at your command, these organs and limbs with which you live—all have been entrusted to you by God, the Almighty, and were given to you in perfect purity and righteousness. If they are afflicted with sin, they become polluted. If, God forbid, they are polluted with that which is forbidden,

---

[46] It is reported from Imam Baqir (AS): There is no servant without a white spot on his heart. When a sin is performed a black spot appears on it. Then if he repents, this blackness is erased. But if he continues to sin, the blackness increases, until it covers the white. When the white is covered, one with such a heart never returns to excellence and goodness. *Usul al-Kafi*, Vol. 3, p. 274, The Book of Faith and Infidelity, the Chapter of Sins, hadith 20.

wickedness results. When the time comes to return this trust, it is possible that you will be asked if this is the right way to protect the trust which was given you. When the trust was placed under your control, was it like this? Was the heart which you were given like this? Were the eyes which were bestowed upon you like this? Were the other organs and limbs which were placed at your will this polluted and dirty? What will be your answer to these questions? How will you meet God when you have committed such treachery with regard to that with which you have been entrusted?

You are young. You have spent your youth in such a way that from a worldly perspective you have given up many benefits. If you use this valuable time and the spring of your youth in the way of God and with a specific sacred purpose, then it has not been wasted, but rather this world and the next have been determined for you. However, if your behavior is of such a manner as is currently witnessed, then you have wasted your youth and the prime of your life has been passed in vain. In the other world, before God, you will be questioned and reproached, while the penalty for your perfidious deeds and acts will not only be limited to the other world. In this world also, various severe difficulties, calamities and troubles will grab you by the neck, and you will fall into the whirlpool of misfortune and disaster.

Another Warning

Your future is dark: numerous enemies are surrounding you on every side and from all strata; dangerous fiendish plans are ready to be enacted which will destroy you and the seminaries. The colonialists dream about what they will do with you; they have deep dreams about what they will do with Islam and the Muslims. With the pretense of Islam, they have drawn up dangerous plans for you. Only in the shade of refinement, preparation and the proper arrangement and order will you be able to push away these corruptions and difficulties, and frustrate the plans of the colonialists. I am now living the last days of my life. Sooner or later I will leave you. But I see before me dark black days ahead for you. If you do not reform and prepare yourselves, and if you do not rule your studies and your lives with order and discipline, then, God forbid, you will be doomed to annihilation. Before you lose the chance, before you fall into the hands of the enemy with regard to every religious and scholarly affair, think! Wake up! Arise!

The first stage is to decide to refine and purify your souls and to reform yourselves.

Prepare and organize yourselves. Establish some order and discipline in the seminaries. Do not let others come to arrange [the affairs of] the seminaries. Do not let others take hold of the seminaries with the excuse that 'these people are not capable of it; it is not their sort of work; they are just a group of loafers who have gathered in the seminaries,' and then in the name of organization and reform, to spoil the seminaries and take you under their own control. Do not give them an excuse. If you are organized and purified, and if in every respect you are well ordered and arranged, others will not be able to aspire to control you. There will then be no way to penetrate into the seminaries and the clerical society. Prepare and purify yourselves. Get ready to prevent the mischief with which you will be faced. Prepare your seminaries for resistance against the events which are to come.

God forbid, black days lie ahead of you. The conditions are ripe for bad days to come. The colonialists want to destroy all aspects of Islam, and you must stand up against them. With love of self and position, with arrogance and pride, you cannot mount any resistance. An evil scholar, a scholar who inclines toward the world, a scholar who thinks of preserving his position and administrative post, will not be able to combat the enemies of Islam. He will be more harmful than others. Take a step for the sake of God. Dispel the love of the world from your heart. Then you will be able to engage in combat. From this moment on, develop and raise this point in your heart, that I must be an armed soldier of Islam, and sacrifice myself for Islam. I must work for Islam until I am destroyed. Do not make excuses for yourself that today is inappropriate. Try to be useful for the future of Islam. In short, become a human being! The colonialists are afraid of human beings. They are afraid of man. The colonialists, who want to plunder all we have, will not allow the training of human beings in religious and scholarly universities. They are afraid of man. If a man is found in a country, it bothers them, and endangers their interests.

It is your duty to make something of yourselves, to become perfect men, and to stand up against the vicious plans of the enemies of Islam. If you are not organized and prepared, if you do not resist and combat the lashes which whip the body of Islam every day, not only will you yourselves be destroyed, but also the precepts and laws of Islam will be annihilated, and you will be responsible. You *'ulama*! You scholars! You Muslims! You will be responsible. First you *'ulama* and seminary students and then the rest of the Muslims will be responsible: "All of you are shepherds and all of you are responsible for tending the flock."[47]You young people must strengthen your wills so that you can stand up against every oppression and injustice. Other than this there is no alternative: your dignity, the dignity of Islam, and the dignity of the Islamic countries depend upon your resistance and opposition.

God Almighty! Protect Islam, the Muslims and the Islamic countries from foreign evils. Cut the hands of the colonialists and traitors to Islam in the Islamic countries and in the

---

[47] *'Awali al-La'alli*, Vol. 1, p. 129, Ch. 8, hadith 3. *Al-Jama' al-Saghir*, Vol. 2, p. 45, 95.

seminaries. Grant success and help to the Islamic *'ulama* and to the great *marja'*[48] in their defense of the sacred laws of the Noble Qur'an and their advancement of the holy ideals of Islam. Make the clergy of Islam aware of their heavy duties and important responsibilities in the present epoch. Protect and keep safe the seminaries and clerical centers from the thievery and influence of the enemies of Islam and the hands of the colonialists. Grant the success of making something of themselves and purifying and refining the soul to the young generation of clerics and university students and to the entire Muslim community. Free the people of Islam from the sleep of negligence, from frailty, from apathy and inflexibility of thought, so that with the lustrous revolutionary teachings of the Qur'an they may come to themselves, rise up, and in the shade of unity and oneness they may cut the hands of the colonialists and of the inveterate enemies of Islam from the Islamic countries, and so that they may regain the freedom, independence, nobility and

---

[48] The *maraji' al-taqlid* are the sources of imitation for Islamic law. [Tr.]

greatness which they have lost. *"Our Lord, pour down upon us patience, and make our steps firm and assist us against the unbelieving people."* (2:250)

The Munajat of the Month of Sha'ban

بِسْمِ ٱللَّهِ ٱلرَّحْمَٰنِ ٱلرَّحِيمِ

Bi-smi llāhi r-Raḥmāni r-Raḥīm

In the Name of Allah, the Merciful, the Compassionate

اَللّٰهُمَّ صَلِّ عَلَىٰ مُحَمَّدٍ وَآلِ مُحَمَّدٍ

allahumma salli `ala muhammadin wa ali muhammadin

O Allah, (please do) send blessings to Muhammad
and the Household of Muhammad,

وَٱسْمَعْ دُعَائِي إِذَا دَعَوْتُكَ

wasma` du`a'i idha da`awtuka

You listen to my supplication whenever I pray to you,

وَٱسْمَعْ نِدَائِي إِذَا نَادَيْتُكَ

wasma` nida'i idha nadaytuka

listen to my call whenever I call upon you,

وَأَقْبِلْ عَلَيَّ إِذَا نَاجَيْتُكَ

wa aqbil `alayya idha najaytuka

and accept from me whenever I make my submission to you in confidence,

فَقَدْ هَرَبْتُ إِلَيْكَ

faqad harabtu ilayka

I have escaped towards you and stood before you,

وَوَقَفْتُ بَيْنَ يَدَيْكَ مُسْتَكِيناً لَكَ

wa waqaftu bayna yadayka mustakinan laka

standing before You, showing submission to You,

مُتَضَرِّعاً إِلَيْكَ

mutadarri`an ilayka

imploring You,

رَاجِياً لِمَا لَدَيْكَ ثَوَابِي

rajiyan lima ladayka thawabi

and hoping for the reward that You have for me.

وَتَعْلَمُ مَا فِي نَفْسِي

wa ta`lamu ma fi nafsi

You know what is in my inner self,

وَتَخْبُرُ حَاجَتِي

wa takhburu hajati

and you are aware of my needs,

وَتَعْرِفُ ضَمِيرِي

wa ta`rifu damiri

and You know what is in my conscience,

وَلاَ يَخْفَىٰ عَلَيْكَ أَمْرُ مُنْقَلَبِي وَمَثْوَايَ

wa la yakhfa `alayka amru munqalabi wa mathwaya

and all my moves and stillness are known by You.

وَمَا أُرِيدُ أَنْ أُبْدِئَ بِهِ مِنْ مَنْطِقِي

wa ma uridu an ubdi'a bihi min mantiqi

So are all the utterances which I want to begin with,

وَأَتَفَوَّهَ بِهِ مِنْ طَلِبَتِي

wa atafawwaha bihi min talibati

all the requests that I want to express,

وَأَرْجُوهُ لِعَاقِبَتِي

wa arjuhu li`aqibati

and all the expectation that I hope for my future.

وَقَدْ جَرَتْ مَقَادِيرُكَ عَلَيَّ يَا سَيِّدِي

wa qad jarat maqadiruka `alayya ya sayyidi

O my Master, all Your decsions in relation
to me have come to pass

فِيمَا يَكُونُ مِنِّي إِلَىٰ آخِرِ عُمْرِي

fima yakunu minni ila akhiri `umri

in all that happens to me up to the end of my
life,

مِنْ سَرِيرَتِي وَعَلَانِيَتِي

min sarirati wa `alaniyati

including my secret and open matters,
shall be experienced by me.

وَبِيَدِكَ لاَ بِيَدِ غَيْرِكَ زِيَادَتِي وَنَقْصِي

*wa biyadika la biyadi ghayrika ziyadati wa
naqsi*

And it is in Your hands, not anybody else's,
that are all my gains and losses

وَنَفْعِي وَضَرِّي

wa naf`i wa darri

and all the benefits and harms that come
upon me.

إِلٰهِي إِنْ حَرَمْتَنِي فَمَنْ ذَا ٱلَّذِي يَرْزُقُنِي

ilahi in haramtani faman dha alladhi yarzuquni

My Lord, if You deprive me (of Your sustenance), then who else can ever provide me with sustenance?

وَإِنْ خَذَلْتَنِي فَمَنْ ذَا ٱلَّذِي يَنْصُرُنِي

wa in khadhaltani faman dha alladhi yansuruni

If You forsake me, then who else will help me?

إِلٰهِي أَعُوذُ بِكَ مِنْ غَضَبِكَ وَحُلُولِ سَخَطِكَ

ilahi a`udhu bika min ghadabika wa hululi sakhatika

My Lord, I do seek Your protection against Your wrath and earning your displeasure.

إِلٰهِي إِنْ كُنْتُ غَيْرَ مُسْتَأْهِلٍ لِرَحْمَتِكَ

ilahi in kuntu ghayra musta'hilin lirahmatika

O my Lord, if I am not deserving of Your mercy,

117

فَأَنْتَ اَهْلُ اَنْ تَجُودَ عَلَيَّ بِفَضْلِ سَعَتِكَ

fa-anta ahlun an tajuda `alayya bifadli sa`atika

You are certainly fit to be generous to me by virtue of your magnanimity.

إِلٰهِي كَأَنِّي بِنَفْسِي وَاقِفَةٌ بَيْنَ يَدَيْكَ

ilahi ka-anni binafsi waqifatun bayna yadayka

My Lord, its like I see myself standing before You

وَقَدْ اَظَلَّهَا حُسْنُ تَوَكُّلِي عَلَيْكَ

wa qad azallaha husnu tawakkuli `alayka

It has been misled by my trust in You,

فَقُلْتَ مَا اَنْتَ اَهْلُهُ وَتَغَمَّدْتَنِي بِعَفْوِكَ

faqulta ma anta ahluhu wa taghammadtani bi`afwika

You said what befitted You and sheltered me with your forgiveness.

إِلٰهِي إِنْ عَفَوْتَ فَمَنْ اَوْلَىٰ مِنْكَ بِذٰلِكَ

ilahi in `afawta faman awla minka bidhalika

My Lord, if you pardon me, then who else is worthier than You are in pardoning.

وَإِنْ كَانَ قَدْ دَنَا أَجَلِي وَلَمْ يُدْنِنِي مِنْكَ عَمَلِي

wa in kana qad dana ajali wa lam yudnini

minka `amali

If my time of death is near and my deeds have

not brought me close to You

فَقَدْ جَعَلْتُ ٱلإِقْرَارَ بِٱلذَّنْبِ إِلَيْكَ وَسِيلَتِي

faqad ja`altu al-iqrara bildhdhanbi ilayka

wasilati

I make this confession of my sins to be

a means of approaching You.

إِلٰهِي قَدْ جُرْتُ عَلَىٰ نَفْسِي فِي ٱلنَّظَرِ لَهَا

ilahi qad jurtu `ala nafsi fi alnnazari laha

My Lord, I have been unjust to my soul

for I have not looked after it;

فَلَهَا ٱلْوَيْلُ إِنْ لَمْ تَغْفِرْ لَهَا

falaha alwaylu in lam taghfir laha

It will be doomed if You do not forgive me.

إِلٰهِي لَمْ يَزَلْ بِرُّكَ عَلَيَّ أَيَّامَ حَيَاتِي

ilahi lam yazal birruka `alayya ayyama

hayati

My Lord, You have never ceased

Your favors from me all my lifetime;

119

فَلاَ تَقْطَعْ بِرَّكَ عَنِّي فِي مَمَاتِي

fala taqta` birraka `anni fi mamati

So do not cease Your goodness

towards me at the time of my death.

إِلٰهِي كَيْفَ اَيَسُ مِنْ حُسْنِ نَظَرِكَ لِي بَعْدَ مَمَاتِي

ilahi kayfa ayasu min husni nazarika li ba`da

mamati

My Lord, how can I despair of Your

benevolent

attention towards me after my death

وَأَنْتَ لَمْ تُوَلِّنِي إِلاّ ٱلْجَمِيلَ فِي حَيَاتِي

wa anta lam tuwallini illa aljamila fi hayati

while You have always been good to me

throughout my lifetime?

إِلٰهِي تَوَلَّ مِنْ أَمْرِي مَا أَنْتَ أَهْلُهُ

ilahi tawalla min amri ma anta ahluhu

My Lord, (please) manage my affairs in the

very way that befits You,

وَعُدْ عَلَيَّ بِفَضْلِكَ عَلَىٰ مُذْنِبٍ قَدْ غَمَرَهُ جَهْلُهُ

wa `ud `alayya bifadlika `ala mudhnibin qad

ghamarahu jahluhu

and confer upon me—a sinful person who is

covered by his ignorance—with Your favors.

إِلٰهِي قَدْ سَتَرْتَ عَلَيَّ ذُنُوباً فِي ٱلدُّنْيَا

ilahi qad satarta `alayya dhunuban fi
alddunya

My Lord, You have concealed my sins in this
world,

وَأَنَا أَحْوَجُ إِلَىٰ سَتْرِهَا عَلَيَّ مِنْكَ فِي ٱلأُخْرَىٰ

wa ana ahwaju ila satriha `alayya minka fi
al-ukhra

but I am in greater need of their being
concealed in the Next Life.

إِذْ لَمْ تُظْهِرْهَا لِأَحَدٍ مِنْ عِبَادِكَ ٱلصَّالِحِينَ

idh lam tuzhirha li-ahadin min `ibadika
alssalihina

You have not revealed my sins even before
any of Your righteous servants;

فَلاَ تَفْضَحْنِي يَوْمَ ٱلْقِيَامَةِ عَلَىٰ رُؤُوسِ ٱلأَشْهَادِ

fala tafdahni yawma alqiyamati `ala ru'usi
al-ashhadi

therefore, (please) do not humuliate me on
the Resurrection Day before all the
witnesses.

إِلَـٰهِي جُودُكَ بَسَطَ أَمَلِي

ilahi juduka basata amali

My Lord, it is Your magnanimity that
expanded my hope,

وَعَفْوُكَ أَفْضَلُ مِنْ عَمَلِي

wa `afwuka afdalu min `amali

and surely Your pardon is superior to my
deeds.

إِلَـٰهِي فَسُرِّنِي بِلِقَائِكَ يَوْمَ تَقْضِي فِيهِ بَيْنَ عِبَادِكَ

*ilahi fasurrani biliqa'ika yawma taqdi fihi
bayna `ibadika*

My Lord, therefore gladden my heart when I
meet You on the day when You shall judge
between Your servants.

إِلَـٰهِي اَعْتِذَارِي إِلَيْكَ اَعْتِذَارُ مَنْ لَمْ يَسْتَغْنِ عَنْ قَبُولِ عُذْرِهِ

*ilahi i`tidhari ilayka i`tidharu man
lam yastaghni `an qabuli `udhrihi*

My Lord, I submit to You the apology of one
who cannot dispense with the acceptance of
his excuse;

فَٱقْبَلْ عُذْرِي يَا أَكْرَمَ مَنِ ٱعْتَذَرَ إِلَيْهِ ٱلْمُسِيئُونَ

faqbal `udhri ya akrama man i`tadhara ilayhi almusi'una

so, (please) accept my excuse, O most Magnanimous of all those before whom the guilty make an apology.

إِلٰهِي لاَ تَرُدَّ حَاجَتِي

ilahi la tarudda hajati

My Lord, (please) do not reject my request,

وَلاَ تُخَيِّبْ طَمَعِي

wa la tukhayyib tama`i

do not dissapoint my hope for You,

وَلاَ تَقْطَعْ مِنْكَ رَجَائِي وَأَمَلِي

wa la taqta` minka raja'i wa amali

and do not cut off from You my hope and expectations from You.

إِلٰهِي لَوْ أَرَدْتَ هَوَانِي لَمْ تَهْدِنِي

ilahi law aradta hawani lam tahdini

My Lord, had You wanted to humiliate me, You would not have guided me (to You).

وَلَوْ أَرَدْتَ فَضِيحَتِي لَمْ تُعَافِنِي

wa law aradta fadihati lam tu`afini

Had You decided to humiliate me,
You would not have excused me.

إلٰهِي مَا أَظُنُّكَ تَرُدُّنِي فِي حَاجَةٍ قَدْ أَفْنَيْتُ عُمْرِي فِي
طَلَبِهَا مِنْكَ

ilahi ma azunnuka tarudduni fi hajatin
qad afnaytu `umri fi talabiha minka

My Lord, I do not expect You to reject my
request that I spent my whole lifetime asking
for it from You.

إلٰهِي فَلَكَ ٱلْحَمْدُ أَبَداً أَبَداً دَائِماً سَرْمَداً

ilahi falaka alhamdu abadan abadan da'iman
sarmadan

My Lord, all praise be to You, forever,
forever, perpetually, everlastingly,

يَزِيدُ وَلاَ يَبِيدُ كَمَا تُحِبُّ وَتَرْضَىٰ

yazidu wa la yabidu kama tuhibbu wa tarda

increasingly, and imperishably, as exactly as
You like and please.

إِلٰهِي إِنْ أَخَذْتَنِي بِجُرْمِي أَخَذْتُكَ بِعَفْوِكَ

ilahi in akhadhtani bijurmi akhadhtuka
bi`afwika

My Lord, if You punish me for my offense,
I shall cling to Your pardon,

وَإِنْ أَخَذْتَنِي بِذُنُوبِي أَخَذْتُكَ بِمَغْفِرَتِكَ

wa in akhadhtani bidhunubi akhadhtuka
bimaghfiratika

if You cease me for my sins, I shall take
hold of Your forgiveness,

وَإِنْ أَدْخَلْتَنِي ٱلنَّارَ أَعْلَمْتُ أَهْلَهَا أَنِّي أُحِبُّكَ

wa in adkhaltani alnnara a`lamtu
ahlaha anni uhibbuka

and if You put me to the fire, I shall declare
to its inmates that I love You.

إِلٰهِي إِنْ كَانَ صَغُرَ فِي جَنْبِ طَاعَتِكَ عَمَلِي

ilahi in kana saghura fi janbi ta`atika `amali

My Lord, should my deeds be insignificant
with respect to obedience to You,

فَقَدْ كَبُرَ فِي جَنْبِ رَجَائِكَ أَمَلِي

faqad kabura fi janbi raja'ika amali

Great indeed is my hope with respect to
my expectations from You.

إلٰهي كَيْفَ أَنْقَلِبُ مِنْ عِنْدِكَ بِٱلْخَيْبَةِ مَحْرُوماً

ilahi kayfa anqalibu min `indika bilkhaybati
mahruman

My Lord, how can it be that I return from
You with disappointment and deprivation

وَقَدْ كَانَ حُسْنُ ظَنِّي بِجُودِكَ أَنْ تَقْلِبَنِي بِٱلنَّجاةِ مَرْحُوماً

wa qad kana husnu zanni bijudika
an taqlibani bilnnajati marhuman

for indeed my beautiful opinion about Your
generosity was that You shall reverse my fate
by savng me mercifully.

إلٰهي وَقَدْ أَفْنَيْتُ عُمْرِي فِي شِرَّةِ ٱلسَّهْوِ عَنْكَ

ilahi wa qad afnaytu `umri fi shirrati
alssahwi `anka

My Lord, I have spent my entire
lifetime in being negligent to You

وَأَبْلَيْتُ شَبَابِي فِي سَكْرَةِ ٱلتَّبَاعُدِ مِنْكَ

wa ablaytu shababi fi sakrati alttaba`udi
minka

and I have spent my whole youth with
the stupor of being distant from You.

إلـٰهي فَلَمْ أَسْتَيْقِظْ أَيَّامَ ٱغْتِرَارِي بِكَ

ilahi falam astayqiz ayyama ightirari bika

My Lord, I did not wake up from my
delusions

وَرُكُوِنـي إِلَىٰ سَبِيلِ سَخَطِكَ

wa rukuni ila sabili sakhatika

and did not desist from pursuing
the path of Your displeasure.

إِلـٰهي وَأَنَا عَبْدُكَ وَٱبْنُ عَبْدِكَ قَائِمٌ بَيْنَ يَدَيْكَ

*ilahi wa ana `abduka wabnu `abdika qa'imun
bayna yadayka*

My Lord, nevertheless, I am—Your servant
and the son of Your servant, now standing
before You

مُتَوَسِّلٌ بِكَرَمِكَ إِلَيْكَ

mutawassilun bikaramika ilayka

and begging You in the name of Your
generosity.

إِلـٰهي أَنَا عَبْدٌ أَتَنَصَّلُ إِلَيْكَ مِمَّا كُنْتُ أُوَاجِهُكَ بِهِ

*ilahi ana `abdun atanassalu ilayka
mimma kuntu uwajihuka bihi*

My Lord, I am a servant, disavowing before
You

127

مِنْ قِلَّةِ اَسْتِحْيَائِي مِنْ نَظَرِكَ

min qillati istihya'i min nazarika

of my past attitude of lack of shame in Your
sight

وَأَطْلُبُ ٱلْعَفْوَ مِنْكَ إِذِ ٱلْعَفْوُ نَعْتٌ لِكَرَمِكَ

*wa atlubu al`afwa minka idh al`afwu na`tun
likaramika*

seek Your pardon as it is the attribute of
Your magnanimty to pardon;

إِلٰهِي لَمْ يَكُنْ لِي حَوْلٌ فَأَنْتَقِلَ بِهِ عَنْ مَعْصِيَتِكَ

*ilahi lam yakun li hawlun fa-antaqila bihi `an
ma`siyatika*

My Lord, I had no strength to desist
from Your disobedience

إِلاّ فِي وَقْتٍ أَيْقَظْتَنِي لِمَحَبَّتِكَ

illa fi waqtin ayqaztani limahabbatika

except when You awakened me for Your love

وَكَمَا أَرَدْتَ أَنْ أَكُونَ كُنْتُ

wa kama aradta an akuna kuntu

Hence, I desired, that I become exactly
as You want me to be.

فَشَكَرْتُكَ بِإِدْخَالِي فِي كَرَمِكَ

fashakartuka bi-idkhali fi karamika

I have thus thanked You, for You
admitting me into Your generosity

وَلِتَطْهِيرِ قَلْبِي مِنْ أَوْسَاخِ ٱلْغَفْلَةِ عَنْكَ

*wa litathiri qalbi min awsakhi alghaflati
`anka*

and You have purified my heart from the
filth of being inattentive to You.

إِلٰهِي ٱنْظُرْ إِلَيَّ نَظَرَ مَنْ نَادَيْتَهُ فَأَجَابَكَ

*ilahi unzur ilayya nazara man nadaytahu fa-
ajabaka*

My Lord, (please) look upon me in the same
way as You have looked at one whom You
called
and he has responded to You

وَٱسْتَعْمَلْتَهُ بِمَعُونَتِكَ فَأَطَاعَكَ

wasta`maltahu bima`unatika fa-ata`aka

and whom You used him in Your service
with Your aid and so he obeys You.

129

يَا قَرِيباً لاَ يَبْعُدُ عَنِ ٱلْمُغْتَرِّ بِهِ

ya qariban la yab`udu `an almughtarri bihi

O the Near one who is not far away
from those who love Him ardently

وَيَا جَوَاداً لاَ يَبْخَلُ عَمَّنْ رَجَا ثَوَابَهُ

*wa ya jawadan la yabkhalu `amman
raja thawabahu*

O He Who is too magnanimous to deprive
one who hopes for His reward!

إِلٰهِي هَبْ لِي قَلْباً يُدْنِيهِ مِنْكَ شَوْقُهُ

ilahi hab li qalban yudnihi minka shawquhu

My Lord, (please) grant me a heart whose
longing
for You will draw one close to You,

وَلِسَاناً يُرْفَعُ إِلَيْكَ صِدْقُهُ

wa lisanan yurfa`u ilayka sidquhu

a tongue whose truthfulness ascends towards
You,

وَنَظَراً يُقَرِّبُهُ مِنْكَ حَقُّهُ

wa nazaran yuqarribuhu minka haqquhu

and a sight whose trueness brings it close to
You.

إِلـٰهِي إِنَّ مَنْ تَعَرَّفَ بِكَ غَيْرُ مَجْهُولٍ

ilahi inna man ta`arrafa bika ghayru majhulin

My Lord, certainly he who recognizes
You shall never be anonymous,

وَمَنْ لاذَ بِكَ غَيْرُ مَخْذُولٍ

wa man ladha bika ghayru makhdhulin

he who seeks Your shelter shall never be
disappointed,

وَمَنْ أَقْبَلْتَ عَلَيْهِ غَيْرُ مَمْلُولٍ

wa man aqbalta `alayhi ghayru mamlulin

and he to whom You turn to does not
fall victim to servility (dejection).

إِلـٰهِي إِنَّ مَنِ ٱنْتَهَجَ بِكَ لَمُسْتَنِيرٌ

ilahi inna man intahaja bika lamustanirun

My Lord, certainly he who abides by
Your Path shall be enlightened,

وَإِنَّ مَنِ ٱعْتَصَمَ بِكَ لَمُسْتَجِيرٌ

wa inna man i`tasama bika lamustajirun

and he who resorts in You finds refuge.

131

وَقَدْ لُذْتُ بِكَ يَا إِلٰهِي فَلاَ تُخَيِّبْ ظَنِّي مِنْ رَحْمَتِكَ

wa qad ludhtu bika ya ilahi fala tukhayyib

zanni min rahmatika

Indeed certainly I have taken shelter in You,
My Lord! So, (please) do not let down my
opinion in Your mercy

وَلاَ تَحْجُبْنِي عَنْ رَأْفَتِكَ

wa la tahjubni `an ra'fatika

and do not exclude me from Your
compassion.

إِلٰهِي أَقِمْنِي فِي أَهْلِ وِلاَيَتِكَ

ilahi aqimni fi ahli wilayatika

My Lord, place me, among those
who show servitude to You,

مُقَامَ مَنْ رَجَا ٱلزِّيَادَةَ مِنْ مَحَبَّتِكَ

muqama man raja alzziyadata min

mahabbatika

the position of those who (incessantly)
hope to increase Your love.

إِلٰهِي وَأَلْهِمْنِي وَلَهاً بِذِكْرِكَ إِلَىٰ ذِكْرِكَ

ilahi wa alhimni walahan bidhikrika

ila dhikrika

My Lord, (please) inspire me with a

mounting

passion for Your rememberance,

وَهِمَّتِي فِي رَوْحِ نَجَاحِ أَسْمَائِكَ وَمَحَلِّ قُدْسِكَ

wa himmati fi rawhi najahi asma'ika wa

mahalli qudsika

and (please) with an ardour for the

refreshing resort to Your names and the

station of Your Holiness.

إِلٰهِي بِكَ عَلَيْكَ إِلاّ أَلْحَقْتَنِي بِمَحَلِّ أَهْلِ طَاعَتِكَ

ilahi bika `alayka illa alhaqtani bimahalli

ahli ta`atika

My Lord, I beseech You in Your name to put

me in the abode of those who are obedient to

You

وَٱلْمَثْوَىٰ ٱلصَّالِحِ مِنْ مَرْضَاتِكَ

walmathwa alssalihi min mardatika

and to the righteous sanctuary of Your good

pleasure,

133

فَإِنِّي لاَ أَقْدِرُ لِنَفْسِي دَفْعاً

fa'inni la aqdiru linafsi daf`an

for I, certainly I have no power to repel any
harm

وَلاَ أَمْلِكُ لَهَا نَفْعاً

wa la amliku laha naf`an

nor to obtain any benefit for it.

إِلٰهِي أَنَا عَبْدُكَ ٱلضَّعِيفُ ٱلْمُذْنِبُ

ilahi ana `abduka aldda`ifu almudhnibu

My Lord, I am Your weak and sinful servant—

وَمَمْلُوكُكَ ٱلْمُنِيبُ

wa mamlukuka almunibu

and Your repenting slave.

فَلاَ تَجْعَلْنِي مِمَّنْ صَرَفْتَ عَنْهُ وَجْهَكَ

fala taj`alni mimman sarafta `anhu wajhaka

So, (please) do not include me amongst those
from whom You have turned away Your face

وَحَجَبَهُ سَهْوُهُ عَنْ عَفْوِكَ

wa hajabahu sahwuhu `an `afwika

and those who are excluded from
Your pardon because of their lapses.

إِلٰهِي هَبْ لِي كَمَالَ ٱلِانْقِطَاعِ إِلَيْكَ

ilahi hab li kamala alinqita'i ilayka

My Lord, (please) grant me absolute devotion
to You

وَأَنِرْ أَبْصَارَ قُلُوبِنَا بِضِيَاءِ نَظَرِهَا إِلَيْكَ

*wa anir absara qulubina bidiya'i
nazariha ilayka*

and illumine the vision of our hearts by the
light of their gaze looking towards You

حَتّىٰ تَخْرِقَ أَبْصَارُ ٱلْقُلُوبِ حُجُبَ ٱلنُّورِ

hatta takhriqa absaru alqulubi hujuba alnnuri

until the vision of our hearts pierces the
curtains of light

فَتَصِلَ إِلَىٰ مَعْدِنِ ٱلْعَظَمَةِ

fatasila ila ma'dini al'azamati

to reach the core of supremacy,

وَتَصِيرَ أَرْوَاحُنَا مُعَلَّقَةً بِعِزِّ قُدْسِكَ

*wa tasira arwahuna mu'allaqatan bi'izzi
qudsika*

and that our souls become suspended by the
majesty of Your Holiness.

إلٰهِي وَٱجْعَلْنِي مِمَّنْ نَادَيْتَهُ فَأَجَابَكَ

ilahi waj`alni mimman nadaytahu fa-ajabaka

My Lord, (please) appoint me of those who
responded to You when You called them,

وَلاحَظْتَهُ فَصَعِقَ لِجَلالِكَ

wa lahaztahu fasa`iqa lijalalika

and at whom You glanced so he swoons
before Your Majesty

فَنَاجَيْتَهُ سِرّاً وَعَمِلَ لَكَ جَهْراً

fanajaytahu sirran wa `amila laka jahran

So You speak to him secretly and he works
for You openly.

إلٰهِي لَمْ أُسَلِّطْ عَلَىٰ حُسْنِ ظَنِّي قُنُوطَ ٱلأَيَاسِ

*ilahi lam usallit `ala husni zanni qunuta al-
ayasi*

My Lord, do not let the dejection of despair
overshadow my beautiful opinion

وَلاَ ٱنْقَطَعَ رَجَائِي مِنْ جَمِيلِ كَرَمِكَ

wa la inqata`a raja'i min jamili karamika

and do not cut my hope from Your generosity

إلٰهِي إِنْ كَانَتِ ٱلْخَطَايَا قَدْ أَسْقَطَتْنِي لَدَيْكَ

*ilahi in kanat alkhataya qad asqatatni
ladayka*

My Lord, if my lapses have made
me to fall from Your grace,

فَٱصْفَحْ عَنِّي بِحُسْنِ تَوَكُّلِي عَلَيْكَ

fasfah `anni bihusni tawakkuli `alayka

So please pardon me for the beauty
of my reliance upon You.

إلٰهِي إِنْ حَطَّتْنِيَ ٱلذُّنُوبُ مِنْ مَكَارِمِ لُطْفِكَ

*ilahi in hattatni aldhdhunubu min makarimi
lutfika*

My Lord, if my wrongdoings have excluded
me from the generosity of Your grace,

فَقَدْ نَبَّهَنِي ٱلْيَقِينُ إِلَىٰ كَرَمِ عَطْفِكَ

faqad nabbahani alyaqinu ila karami `atfika

So certainly my conviction reassures me
of Your generosity and gentleness.

إِلٰهِي إِنْ أَنَامَتْنِيَ ٱلْغَفْلَةُ عَنِ ٱلِاسْتِعْدَادِ لِلِقَائِكَ

ilahi in anamatni alghaflatu `an alisti`dadi
liliqa'ika

My Lord, if my neglect has lulled me into
slumber preventing me from preparing
myself for my meeting with You,

فَقَدْ نَبَّهَتْنِي ٱلْمَعْرِفَةُ بِكَرَمِ ٱلَآئِكَ

faqad nabbahatni alma`rifatu bikarami
ala'ika

So certainly my recognition apprises me of
Your generous bounties has awakened me.

إِلٰهِي إِنْ دَعَانِي إِلَىٰ ٱلنَّارِ عَظِيمُ عِقَابِكَ

ilahi in da`ani ila alnnari `azimu `iqabika

My Lord, if Your grave chastisement
calls me to the Hellfire,

فَقَدْ دَعَانِي إِلَىٰ ٱلْجَنَّةِ جَزِيلُ ثَوَابِكَ

faqad da`ani ila aljannati jazilu thawabika

So Your plentious reward has called me to
Paradise.

إِلٰهِي فَلَكَ أَسْأَلُ وَإِلَيْكَ أَبْتَهِلُ وَأَرْغَبُ

ilahi falaka as'alu wa ilayka abtahilu wa arghabu

My Lord, so to You I beg and I implore and I request.

وَأَسْأَلُكَ أَنْ تُصَلِّيَ عَلَىٰ مُحَمَّدٍ وَآلِ مُحَمَّدٍ

wa as'aluka an tusalliya `ala muhammadin wa ali muhammadin

I beseech You to bless Muhammad and the Household of Muhammad

وَأَنْ تَجْعَلَنِي مِمَّنْ يُدِيمُ ذِكْرَكَ

wa an taj`alani mimman yudimu dhikraka

and to include me with those who always remember You,

وَلاَ يَنْقُضُ عَهْدَكَ

wa la yanqudu `ahdaka

and those who never break their promise to You,

وَلاَ يَغْفُلُ عَنْ شُكْرِكَ

wa la yaghfulu `an shukrika

and who do not neglect to thank You,

وَلاَ يَسْتَخِفُّ بِأَمْرِكَ

wa la yastakhiffu bi-amrika

and who never belittle Your commands.

إِلٰهِي وَأَلْحِقْنِي بِنُورِ عِزِّكَ ٱلْأَبْهَجِ

ilahi wa alhiqni binuri `izzika al-abhaji

My Lord, (please do) submerge me in the
most
blissful lights of Your majesty,

فَأَكُونَ لَكَ عَارِفاً

fa-akuna laka `arifan

so that I will recognize You

وَعَنْ سِوَاكَ مُنْحَرِفاً

wa `an siwaka munharifan

and renounce all else except You,

وَمِنْكَ خَائِفاً مُرَاقِباً

wa minka kha'ifan muraqiban

and that I will be fearful of and careful with
You.

يَا ذَا ٱلْجَلَلِ وَٱلإِكْرَامِ

ya dha aljalali wal-ikrami

O Lord of Majesty and Honor!

140

وَصَلَّىٰ ٱللَّهُ عَلَىٰ مُحَمَّدٍ رَسُولِهِ وَآلِهِ ٱلطَّاهِرِينَ

wa salla allahu `ala muhammadin rasulihi wa alihi alttahirina

May Allah send blessings to Muhammad, His Messenger, and upon his Household the Infallible,

وَسَلَّمَ تَسْلِيماً كَثِيراً

wa sallama tasliman kathiran

and may countless greetings be to them.

141

CPSIA information can be obtained
at www.ICGtesting.com
Printed in the USA
BVHW091323290522
638419BV00002BC/122

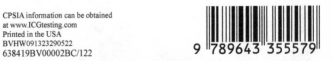